PRAISE FOR
THE GLUTEN-FREE KITCHEN

"An excellent source of gluten-free recipes that taste good and are easy to prepare. With recipes for entrees, cakes, pies, puddings, muffins, and many other foods, as well as lists of gluten-free support groups and suppliers, this book will be welcomed by anyone who wants to prepare delicious food without gluten."

—Suzanne R. Curtis, Ph.D., R.D., department of Nutrition and Food Science, University of Maryland

"The conversational tone of this book makes you feel like your friend is in the kitchen lending a hand. Roben helps make gluten-free cooking easy. Except for three basic 'gluten-free' ingredients most of the other ingredients are already in your kitchen. This book offers a wealth of tips and helpful hints for successful gluten-free cooking . . . including recipes most of us grew up enjoying."

—Cynthia R. Kupper, C.R.D., executive director of the Gluten Intolerance Group

"Snickerdoodles! An old family favorite I can enjoy again. And buttermilk loaf—soft, sliceable, and easy!"

—Elaine Smith, gluten allergy sufferer

The Gluten-Free Kitchen

Over 135 Delicious Recipes for People with Gluten Intolerance or Wheat Allergy

Roben Ryberg

THREE RIVERS PRESS • NEW YORK

Published by Three Rivers Press, New York, New York. Member of the Crown Publishing Group, a division of Random House, Inc.
www.crownpublishing.com

Originally published by Prima Publishing, Roseville, California, in 2000.

NUTRITIONAL ANALYSES
A per serving nutritional breakdown is provided for each recipe. If a range is given for an ingredient amount, the breakdown is based on the smaller number. If a range is given for servings, the breakdown is based on the larger number. If a choice of ingredients is given in an ingredient listing, the breakdown is calculated using the first choice. Nutritional content may vary depending on the specific brands or types of ingredients used. "Optional" ingredients or those for which no specific amount is stated are not included in the breakdown. Nutritional figures are rounded to the nearest whole number.

Roben sold Miss Roben's Gluten-Free Foods in 1992. She is not affiliated with her successors.

Recipes on the cover are: Biscuits (page 75), Rolled Sugar Cookies (page 196), Fried Chicken (page 52), and Strawberry Pie (page 228).

Printed in the United States of America

Library of Congress Cataloging-in-Publication Data
Ryberg, Roben E.
The gluten-free kitchen : over 135 delicious recipes for people with gluten intolerance or wheat allergy / by Roben E. Ryberg.
p. cm.
Includes index.
1. Gluten-free diet—recipes. I. Title
RM237.86.R93 2000
641.5'63—dc21 00-028562
CIP

ISBN 0-7615-2272-7

10 9 8 7

First Edition

To God, for my blessings.

To my husband, for his unconditional love.

And to my children, my best blessing.

Contents

Foreword, by Peter H.R. Green, M.D. xiii
Preface, by Stephanie L. Brina-Herres, M.S., R.D. xvi
Acknowledgments xix
Introduction xx

1. The Gluten-Free Baker's Pantry 1

2. Breakfast 13

Bagels 14
Buttermilk Pancakes 16
Cake Doughnuts 18
Chipped Beef Gravy 20
Cinnamon-Raisin Biscuits 22
Coffee Cake 24
Danish 26
French Toast 28
Pancakes 29
Sausage Gravy 30
Raised Doughnuts 32
Sour Cream Breakfast Muffins 34
Sourdough Pancakes 36
Special Waffles 38
Waffles 39
Streusel Cake 40

3. Lunch and Dinner 43

Chicken Rice Soup 44
Chicken Breast with Wine and Mushrooms 46

Chicken Pot Pie 48
Chili 50
Fried Chicken 52
Ham and Cheese Pocket Pies 54
Marinated Grilled Chicken 56
Meat Loaf 57
Onion Rings 58
Roast Beef with Gravy 59
Pork Scallopini 60
Pizza 62
Quiche 64
Stuffing 66
Beef Vegetable Soup 67
Seafood Crepes 68
Shepherd's Pie 70

4. Breads 73

Biscuits 75
All-Purpose Loaf 76
Buttermilk Loaf 78
Bread Sticks 80
Cheese Straws 82
Cinnamon Loaf 84
Cinnamon Rolls 86
Cornbread—Version 1 88
Cornbread—Version 2 89
Cottage Dill Loaf 90
Chocolate Bread 92
Egg Bread Loaf 94

English Muffins 96
Focaccia 98
Hot Cross Buns 100
Pizza Crust 102
Rolls 104
Sourdough Loaf 106

5. Quick Breads 109

Apple Muffins 110
Banana Bread 112
Banana Muffins 114
Blueberry Muffins 116
Cranberry-Orange Bread 118
Nut Bread 120
Pumpkin Bread 122
Pumpkin Spice Muffins 124
Applesauce Quick Bread 126
Savory Hush Puppies 127
Strawberry Shortcake 128
Sweet Biscuits 129
Zucchini Bread 130
Sweet Hush Puppies 132

6. Cakes 133

Buttercream Icing 135
Angel Food Cake 136
Boston Cream Pie 138
Carrot Cake 140
Chocolate Buttercream Icing 142

Chocolate Pound Cake 143
Chocolate Cake 144
Chocolate Angel Food Cake 146
Chocolate Velvet Icing 148
Gingerbread 150
Pecan Cake 152
Petite Chocolate Cake 153
Petite Yellow Cake 154
Pound Cake 155
Pineapple Upside-Down Cake 156
Red Velvet Cake 158
Simply Sinful Chocolate Cake 160
Spice Snacking Cake 162
Sponge Cake 164
Velvet Icing 166
Yellow Cake 168

7. Cookies 169

Brownies 170
Burnt-Edge Wafers 172
Cheesecake Brownies 174
Chocolate Chip Cookies 176
Chocolate Drops 178
Crispy Sugar Cookies 180
Pecan Meringues 181
Double Chocolate Cookies 182
Gingersnaps 184
Ladyfingers 186
Lemon Cookie Bars 188
Lemon Sugar Cookies 190

Peanut Butter Cookies 192
Raisin Spice Cookies 194
Rolled Sugar Cookies 196
Shortbread Cookies 198
Snickerdoodles 200
Spritz 202
Toffee Bars 204
Vanilla Wafers 206

8. Pies and Tarts 207

Apple Pie 208
Blueberry Tart 210
Cherry Pie 212
Chocolate Meringue Pie 214
Apple Tart 216
Cookie Crumb Crust 217
Custard Pie 218
Pumpkin Pie 219
Key Lime Pie 220
Lemon Meringue Pie 222
Peach Streusel Pie 224
Pecan Pie 226
Strawberry Pie 228
Turnovers 230
Traditional Piecrust 232
Sweet Pastry Crust 234

9. Other Sweets 235

Apple Crisp 236
Apple Fritters 238

Baked Custard 240
Banana Pudding 242
Blueberry Cobbler 244
Cheesecake 246
Chocolate Cheesecake 248
Chocolate Pudding 250
Meringue 251
Peach Cobbler 252
Rice Pudding 254
Crepes 256
Funnel Cake 258
Ice Cream Cones 260
Streusel 262
Vanilla Pudding 263
Whipped Cream 264

Appendix: Gluten-Free Resources 265
Index 275
International Conversion Chart 283

Foreword

Roben Ryberg's book, *The Gluten-Free Kitchen,* fills a void for people with gluten intolerance. There are only a few books on the market that can provide information of the quality found in this book. Gluten intolerance is manifested as gluten sensitive enteropathy or celiac disease. Another manifestation is the intensely itchy rash of dermatitis herpetiformis. Dermatitia herpetiformis, or DH, can be regarded as celiac disease of the skin. The offending agents or environmental precipitants of these diseases are the gliadin proteins found in the gluten of wheat. There are similar proteins which have identical toxic effects found in barley and rye. Oats lack these proteins, however, they are contaminated at all stages of production, storage, and milling with grains containing gluten.

Gluten sensitive enteropathy, or celiac disease, is a lifelong illness. Treatment is directed at eliminating gluten from the diet. Luckily, this is not a sentence to a life of unappetizing, unpleasant tasting meals. As one can see from the high-quality, variable cakes, breads, and other foods described in this book, the gluten-free diet can be as varied, and without question healthier, than a regular diet.

Celiac disease is regarded by most physicians as an uncommon disease in the United States. This is very different from the picture in many countries of the world where celiac disease is regarded as a common entity. This is particularly so in areas of Europe including Ireland, North Europe, and Italy. It is therefore somewhat surprising that the disease is considered rare in the U.S. when the populations of the United States and Europe share common genetic origins. The supposed rarity of the disease in the United States is probably a reflection of a shift to a more silent form of the disease together with the failure of physician recognition. Recent screening studies using highly sensitive antibody blood tests have demonstrated a similar prevalence of the disease in the U.S. to that found in Europe. With increasing education and recognition by physicians, there will no doubt be a larger segment of the population being advised to adopt a gluten-free diet.

If a diagnosis of celiac disease or dermatitis herpetiformis is established, the gluten-free diet must be adhered to for life. The reason for this is the increased rate of malignancies associated with celiac disease. This increased rate returns to that of the normal population after at least five years on a gluten-free diet. In addition, recent data have demonstrated that the earlier the diagnosis and the earlier a patient can commence a gluten-free diet, the fewer other autoimmune-type diseases the patient will acquire. Therefore, there is compelling evidence that once a diagnosis is made, patients should remain on the gluten-free diet. Frequently when a gluten-free diet is adhered to, there is an increased feeling of well-being and a reduction in presenting symptoms. These symptoms have often been present for many years and have been attributed to an irritable bowl syndrome, chronic fatigue syndrome, or fibromyalgia.

Another important factor in the management of patients with celiac disease is screening family members. It is well established that at least 10 percent of family members will have the disease even if they are asymptomatic. A diagnosis of celiac disease is suggested by serological or antibody testing. An intestinal biopsy, however, remains the gold standard for diagnosis. A biopsy is important because a few patients may not respond to a gluten-free diet, and subsequent biopsies are necessary to be compared to the original baseline biopsy. Strict criteria for diagnosis should be adhered to. Commencing the diet without a definitive diagnosis often leads to initial improvement in symptoms. Symptoms may recur prompting further withdrawal of other foods. Finally, patients are left totally confused about what they can eat. There are some individuals who are wheat intolerant and do not have celiac disease. These individuals are probably in the minority.

The majority of patients, once on a gluten-free diet, will enjoy normal good health. However, it is recommended that antibody testing be performed at regular intervals in case gluten is being ingested unintentionally. This may well be in the form of medications which can contain wheat starch as the inert filler.

The usual instructions of the diagnosing physician are for the patient to either consult a nutritionist or research a gluten-free diet from the Internet. Unfortunately, both of these approaches have drawbacks. Few dieticians or nutritionists are adequately educated in the intricacies of a strict gluten-free diet. In addition, the plethora of information available on the Internet to patients is daunting and frequently confusing. Patients with celiac disease should avoid wheat, barley, rye, and oats. There is a considerable amount of misinformation on various sites on the Internet in which patients with celiac disease are advised to avoid other food substances and additives. This is without scientific basis.

There is no doubt that resources such as this book, *The Gluten-Free Kitchen,* are an important adjunct to any household which is attempting to be gluten free. I must congratulate Roben on her superb effort.

Peter H.R. Green, M.D.
Clinical Professor of Medicine
Columbia University College of
Physicians and Surgeons
New York, New York

Preface

Coping with a special diet, particularly a gluten-free diet, is never easy, but Roben Ryberg's new book, *The Gluten-Free Kitchen,* can help to make it a little easier for anyone with celiac sprue. It features a wide variety of recipes that use many readily accessible ingredients along with instructions that are relatively easy to follow. Roben tries to limit the number of specialty ingredients a reader of the book would need to purchase in order to prepare a broad selection of recipes from the cookbook.

The strength of the cookbook lies in the wealth of scratch baked goods recipes that can enable anyone willing to experiment even a little in the kitchen to have more options for such foods than commercial sources provide. Knowledge is power, and the recipes Roben provides are empowering for anyone coping with gluten enteropathy or cooking for someone else in an effort to improve the quality of their life on a gluten-free diet.

Don't let the cover fool you—although it shows high-fat foods such as biscuits, pie crust, cookies, and fried chicken, there are recipes which are lower in fat in the book as well. There are recipes that use a pasteurized, powdered, shelf stable egg white product which is a personal fat-free favorite of mine to use in all sorts of recipes with very satisfactory results.

Roben writes her recipes in a non-threatening style, so that even a novice in the kitchen should feel that he or she can give at least a few recipes a try and achieve reasonable success. Personal anecdotes sprinkled throughout the cookbook add a warm touch to Roben's writing style and make it easier to do what she asks each and every reader to do—trust her judgment in the choices she has made in each recipe's ingredients. Even though she is not a food scientist, Roben includes some helpful tips on how a variety of those ingredients function in baking. Such information can be very useful to any new explorer in the realm of gluten-free cooking.

As a nutritionist, part of my job is to help people come to terms with a special diet. That's often easier said than done. Finding helpful tools that will meet a number of different individuals' needs on a special diet restriction can be a difficult task at times. *The Gluten-Free Kitchen* is a promising addition to the gluten-free toolbox for use by many individuals who want access to additional resources in the effort to manage their gluten enteropathy. Instead of relying on rice-based recipes, Roben has chosen to ally herself with other starch options of corn and potato in the majority of her recipes. She also features two gums in some recipes: xanthan gum to a greater extent and guar gum to a lesser extent, thereby allowing additional textures to be incorporated throughout the cookbook's eight specific recipe chapters. Her introductory remarks and first chapter explain her mission and focus well.

Anyone with a sweet tooth is bound to find a recipe to suit his or her fancy, and needs only to remember the wise old adage of consuming choices in moderation. From once-in-a-while breakfast treats to pies, cookies, cakes, as well as other sweets, there are many tempting items to shatter the perceived monotony usually associated with following a special diet. There is a selection of breads as well to help round out the prepared starch options in the diet, which is all important. Bringing variety to the starch consumption of someone living gluten-free is a crusade in and of itself!

The Gluten Free Kitchen will help to fill a void in the bookshelf of those persons searching for recipes for both gluten-free everyday bread items as well as occasional sweet treats and wants those choices to expand beyond rice-based recipes or commercial products. And when it comes to special diets, choice and options are what it's all about.

Much success with the book!

Healthy Regards,

Stephanie Brina-Herres, MS, RD, CDN, CFCS
Creative Nutrition Concepts

Acknowledgments

A special thank you to the celiac community for welcoming me back, and especially Bea Newell, who I am proud to call my friend; Cynthia Kupper, C.R.D., for her ingredient expertise; Cathy Berger, for her relentless taste analysis; Lee Permenter, for unscrambling my words; and Joslyn Mock, for believing in this project.

Introduction

Welcome to the gluten-free kitchen!

If you're missing wheat and all its subtleties or you're just looking to expand your gluten-free baking, you've found the right place. In this book, you will find many cakes, cookies, and quick breads indistinguishable from their wheat-containing counterparts. Our yeast breads are mild, pleasant, palatable substitutes for wheat breads. And our entrees will be enjoyed by all. These recipes have been tested and praised by individuals with and without special dietary needs.

This book does not follow the "rice is best" approach to gluten-free baking. Instead, cornstarch and potato starch are used as its primary "flours." With these recipes, you will achieve better results, need fewer special ingredients, and use less fat, sugar, and eggs for comparable foods.

If you've eaten it and it contained wheat, it's probably in this book. From Ice Cream Cones to Bagels to Onion Rings, it's here.

I began gluten-free baking nearly ten years ago to rescue a friend from her very restrictive gluten-free diet. That adventure eventually led to the founding of Miss Roben's Gluten-Free Foods and, with it, a long-lasting love of manipulating gluten-free flours into "real" food.

If you could ask me what to try first, I would suggest one of my favorites: Buttermilk Pancakes, Breadsticks, Orange/Cranberry Bread, Carrot Cake, or Fried Chicken. I trust that you will soon be a believer, like me, and that you may truly enjoy all the food you've been missing.

CHAPTER 1

The Gluten-Free Baker's Pantry

Because gluten can be hiding where you would least expect, together we'll walk through all ingredients used in this book. I have tried my best to keep ingredients simple, safe, and familiar. Because manufacturers sometimes change ingredients from one production run to the next, it is crucial to read the ingredients of all food products each time you shop. After a short time, you will quickly recognize foods that need extra-close scrutiny.

It is important that your gluten-free baking supplies not come in contact with gluten-containing foods, flours, surfaces, or utensils that have not been thoroughly cleaned. It is also a good idea to purchase only sealed packages to further protect against cross-contamination.

To better evaluate your food choices, becoming involved in one of the national and/or local celiac support groups is extremely helpful. These groups often research product content and manufacturing procedures to locate trace amounts of gluten. They also have restaurant guides, newsletters, and other useful materials. It is also possible to research food choices on the Internet at www.glutenfreeinfo.com and other gluten-free Web sites. While product labels contain good information, ingredient information is sometimes insufficient for complete gluten content evaluation. The national organizations are listed in the appendix of this book, along with gluten-free suppliers and information of special interest.

Ingredients

Flours—cornstarch, potato starch, and cornmeal

A number of other "flours" are acceptable to a gluten-free diet, including rice, tapioca, and soy and other beans. Rice flours can make for a gritty texture. Tapioca flour can be a bit expensive, and soy flour has a strong flavor. Other bean flours are not as readily available and can cause gas. Additionally, making really tasty baked goods with some of these flours requires using more fats, sugars, and eggs than are used for recipes in this book.

You may be wondering why I use principally cornstarch and potato starch. There are three reasons: (1) these flours are wonderful for re-creating the flavor and texture of traditional baked goods, (2) they are easy to find, and (3) they are modestly priced. Cornstarch is located in the baking aisle of your local grocery store. Potato starch is found in the kosher and/or baking sections of many grocery stores. It can also be found at most health food stores and in nearly all oriental markets. And you can always order flours from one of the fine gluten-free mail-order suppliers listed in the appendix of this book.

A number of flours simply must be avoided: wheat, rye, oat, barley, and spelt. Some debate simmers over whether certain other flours may be used by gluten-intolerant individuals, including amaranth, buckwheat, millet, teff, and quinoa. In my opinion, until any flour is widely endorsed by the celiac community, do not include it in your diet. It's just not worth the risk.

Fats—shortening, vegetable oil, butter, nonstick spray

I do not use margarine in this book because some contain unacceptable ingredients, and oil-water ratios vary by brand. The mono- and diglycerides in shortening are acceptable. But, again, look closely at all labels. The annatto coloring added seasonally to butter has been troublesome for some in the gluten-free community because wheat may be used as an extender in the manufacturing process. I suggest you avoid annatto since it is easy to find butter without it.

I like olive oil and use it to sauté onions in the focaccia. However, olive oil is too strongly flavored for baking, and it does not enhance the flavor of the breads in this book. Look carefully at the label of nonstick sprays for alcohol content to learn whether it is unacceptably grain based.

Sugars—brown sugar, white sugar, powdered sugar, molasses, light corn syrup, honey

Most brown sugars consist of sugar and molasses, which are fine. Be careful of any other ingredients, especially caramel coloring. Unrefined sugars are certainly a good alternative. You must also exercise care in buying corn syrup because flavorings may be of an unknown source. Karo brand corn syrup currently uses pure vanilla, which is acceptable to use. Remember that ingredients can change at any time, so it is wise to contact manufacturers with any questions on gluten content.

Leavening—baking powder, baking soda, yeast

Generally speaking, most brands of these items are fine. I use Red Star yeast, Calumet and Rumford baking powders, and Arm & Hammer baking soda.

Stabilizers/gums—cream of tartar, xanthan gum, guar gum

In this book, cream of tartar is used only to stabilize beaten egg whites. Xanthan and/or guar gums are used to duplicate the texture of traditional baked goods. They replace the gluten (the stretchy stuff) found in wheat flour. Without such a "binder," most gluten-free baked goods would simply crumble. While xanthan gum and guar gum are sometimes used interchangeably in gluten-free baking, I do not do so in this book. Using guar creates a spongier texture (like in cakes) while xanthan creates a stretchier texture (best for breads). Xanthan is also used when more body is desired in a batter.

Xanthan and guar gums are used extensively in foods today. Many traditional cake mixes, ice creams, salad dressings, and numerous other food products contain them. Please do not shy away from baking because of the need to use these gums.

Guar gum is known to be a mild laxative. While eating an entire batch of cookies could cause a bit of gastric distress, moderate portions are usually well tolerated. However, should you be an individual sensitive to guar gum, please substitute xanthan gum in these recipes at 3/4 teaspoon xanthan for each 1 teaspoon guar. In nearly all recipes, you will find this substitution very workable.

Xanthan and guar gums are available at many health food stores and through many of the suppliers and support groups listed in the appendix.

Dairy—milk, buttermilk, cottage cheese, cream cheese, unflavored yogurt, cheddar cheese, parmesan cheese, evaporated milk, sour cream

Most of these items do not cause the celiac concern. However, yellow-colored cheddar cheese usually contains annatto, so please opt for white cheddar cheese in its place. Nearly all major brands of cottage cheese contain modified food starch, and some even contain colorings. Modified food starch may contain wheat. My label reading shows, however, that some store brands of cottage cheese do not contain modified food starch or colorings—a much better choice.

Juices—lime juice, lemon juice, key lime juice, orange juice

Eggs—large eggs, Just Whites

Just Whites is the brand of pasteurized egg whites that I like to use for meringue. It may be found in most markets and health food stores. If you have trouble locating it, check the specialty food suppliers listed in the appendix.

Flavorings—vanilla flavoring, lemon flavoring

Many flavorings contain alcohol and/or caramel coloring. Even vanilla extract contains alcohol. This alcohol may or may not be unacceptably grain based. And because some caramel coloring contains gluten it should be avoided or its origin known before use. For flavorings, it is better to purchase those labeled "gluten-free" from health-food stores or specialty mail-order suppliers listed in the appendix of this book.

Nuts and other miscellaneous foods—cocoa, unsweetened chocolate, coconut, semisweet chocolate chips, red and green food colorings, peanut butter

Most ingredients in each of these food items are usually fine for the celiac. However, all food labels should be read carefully for hidden gluten. At this writing, I use Baker's Angel Flake Coconut, Baker's Semi-Sweet Chocolate Chips, and/or Nestle Semi-Sweet Chocolate Morsels for my gluten-free baking. Most, if not all, major brands of peanut butter contain rapeseed oil and monoglycerides. Rapeseed, which has not been as thoroughly researched as other grains, does not seem to be a concern to the gluten-free diet. And the monoglycerides are acceptable in a product like this. Natural peanut butters usually contain only peanuts. If you don't mind stirring your peanut butter before use, it is certainly the safest choice.

I am not especially fond of food colorings, but green Key Lime Pie and red Red Velvet Cake are more attractive. While these colorings are not a dietary concern, you may omit the colorings if you like.

Spices and herbs—salt, cinnamon, nutmeg, ginger, sage, oregano, rosemary, bay leaf, basil, Jane's Crazy Mixed-Up Salt, pepper, red pepper, dill weed, fresh garlic, red pepper, coriander, cumin

Processing herbs and spices, especially blends, sometimes involves the use of gluten-containing grains. It is important to know that the manufacturing process is safe. Be especially cautious of extenders or flow agents listed on the labels of these products. It is always a good idea to contact the manufacturer for processing information. Remember, though, that procedures can change—be careful. Jane's Crazy Mixed-Up Salt is currently processed without gluten. It is my favorite all-purpose spice blend.

Whole grains—rice

Rice is the only whole grain used in this book. It is only used for rice pudding and chicken rice soup.

Vinegar—apple cider vinegar

Apple cider vinegar is my choice for baking. Distilled vinegar is thought acceptable, although its possible grain distillation still makes some people hesitant to use it.

Wine—dry white wine

In several dinner entrées I use dry white wine for the sauce. I generally use a nice California table wine.

Fresh and frozen fruits—apples, peaches, raisins, sour cherries, blueberries, strawberries, orange zest, cranberries, bananas

Canned fruits—applesauce, pumpkin, pineapple, maraschino cherries, jam

The only fruit used in this book that may cause concern is maraschino cherries. Some are fine; just check the label. Be ready for a long list of unusual ingredients and keep a special watch for suspect flavorings.

Fresh and frozen vegetables—onions, mushrooms, zucchini, carrots, red bell peppers, mixed frozen vegetables

Canned vegetables—tomato paste, black beans

Contadina tomato paste currently contains just tomatoes. Other brands contain spices and flavorings whose gluten content is not known.

Meats—chipped beef, sausage, ham, chicken, pork, beef

Chipped beef can contain brown sugar. Because the ingredients of the brown sugar are not listed on the label, you cannot be absolutely sure the chipped beef is risk-free unless verified by the manufacturer. Some brands do not use brown sugar.

Some ingredients may be of concern in sausage. Look for sausages with a few simple, known ingredients. Jimmy Dean currently uses no gluten in the processing/production of any of its fresh pork sausage.

Equipment

No special equipment is needed for gluten-free baking, but a few kitchen essentials will help immensely.

- **Hand-held or stand mixer**—A mixer will help fully incorporate the gluten-free flours into the batter. Flour clumps are unlikely to dissolve during baking. Because very few of the batters/doughs here are heavy or "difficult," a modest mixer is just fine for nearly all recipes in this book.
- **Measuring cups**—Good measuring cups are important. Being off just a little bit can make a big difference in your baking results. These cups need not be expensive, just clearly marked.
- **Measuring spoons**—Good quality measuring spoons are probably the most important gluten-free baking tool. Some ingredients are measured by just 1/4 teaspoon, and if that ingredient is a binding agent, for example, mismeasuring even slightly can mean the difference between a gummy dessert and a delicious dessert.
- **Rubber spatulas**—Gluten-free batters tend to stick to the sides of mixing bowls. Rubber spatulas are wonderful for scraping down the sides of the bowl.
- **Waxed paper and freezer bags**—Waxed paper is really great for rolling out pie crusts. And since most gluten-free baked goods are best stored in the freezer, you'll need a supply of freezer bags.
- **No bread machines**—Lots of gluten-free bakers use bread machines. They work extremely well with rice-based formulas, but they simply overbake my recipes, making for unpleasant results. Moreover, the strong mixing power of a bread machine is not needed. And why wait 4 hours for a bread machine to bake a loaf of bread when my recipes take only minutes to mix and bake in 35 minutes or less?

Techniques

This book does not always follow traditional baking methods. None of the baking steps is difficult, just a little different. It is important to follow the directions closely. Ingredients are used for very specific results in the final baked goods.

Not only are my methods sometimes different but batters and doughs will often look quite different, too. Finished baked goods will, however, look (not to mention taste) remarkably like traditional baked goods. Please do not adjust any recipes because they look odd during the mixing process. Trust me.

Regarding Substitutions

- **Milk**—In many cases, skim milk, soy milk, or rice milk can be used cup for cup in place of cow's milk. These substitutions will alter the taste of the finished baked goods; only you can decide whether you like the results. Also know that many individuals who cannot eat dairy when first diagnosed with gluten intolerance grow to tolerate it months later.
- **Wine**—Wine is used in several dinner entrées. Should you prefer not to use wine, substitute 1 cup water and 1 tablespoon lemon juice for each cup of wine.
- **Fats**—Please do not substitute the fats called for in these recipes unless absolutely necessary. Each fat has unique baking characteristics. Even the small amounts sometimes used are for very specific purposes.
- **Eggs**—In many cases, egg substitutes work just fine. The final taste will, of course, be a bit different.
- **Xanthan and guar gums**—In many cases xanthan can be substituted for guar gum. A scant 3/4 teaspoon of xanthan can be used for each 1 teaspoon guar. Substituting guar for xanthan is more difficult, as xanthan has been used to achieve very specific textures in batters and doughs. You may be able to substitute guar for xanthan in loaf breads, but not in any doughs that need to be shaped, rolled, or

used to support the weight of other ingredients, because the new doughs will be too thin to achieve these results.

Two newly available alternatives to xanthan and guar are now available. They are carrageenan (a special formulation of seaweed extract) and karaya gum (from the sap of the Stericulia urens tree, grown mostly in India). Carrageenan may be substituted at 1/3 teaspoon for each 1 teaspoon xanthan and at 1/4 teaspoon for each 1 teaspoon guar. Carrageenan has the unique ability to more than double the moisture-life of baked goods. Karaya may be substituted at 1/2 teaspoon for each 1 teaspoon xanthan and at a scant 1/2 teaspoon for each 1 teaspoon guar. These substitution ratios are specific to the type of karaya and carrageenan as supplied by Gluten Free Essentials, listed in the appendix.

You may ask why karaya gum and carrageenan are not used in these recipes. It is because xanthan and guar are the current industry standards. Xanthan and guar are terrific, but these alternatives can provide as good or better results at approximately half the cost per use of xanthan

Storage

Gluten-free baked goods dry out more quickly than their wheat-containing counterparts, so wrap them well once they have cooled. These foods need refrigeration or freezing to extend their shelf life. Refrigeration or freezing also helps maintain the texture and moisture level of your baked goods. Recipes for more sensitive foods have a reminder to refrigerate or freeze, but if you are ever in doubt, freeze those extra servings.

One Final Word of Caution

Maintaining a gluten-free diet is essential to the good health of a gluten-intolerant person. Eating gluten-containing foods (call it cheating) is dangerous—period. External wellness can mask internal damage.

If you're like most gluten-intolerant individuals, you've spent a long time feeling ill and seeking a correct diagnosis. Now, you've been given a great opportunity to feel good! Please take the time necessary to read food labels, join a support group, and ensure you buy safe ingredients. My writing and baking styles are lighthearted, but staying gluten-free is serious.

While I hope that this book returns joy to your eating, I cannot tell you that this book is the answer to all your food concerns. Other allergies, medical conditions, and hidden gluten can contribute to ongoing difficulties. Please discuss any such frustrations with your doctor.

And, once your shopping is done, please spend a little more time with me, making food that will make you feel good—like Cookies and Milk! Pizza! Chocolate Cake! Strawberry Pie!

CHAPTER 2

Breakfast

So, how long has it been since you've had a fresh doughnut? Too long, I'll bet. Whereas traditional raised (yeast) doughnuts take hours to make, mine take only minutes and are every bit as delicious.

This chapter will bring you back to the breakfast table. You will find the Special Waffles to be among the best you've ever eaten—and I mean before or after your dietary restrictions. The whole family will enjoy the Buttermilk Pancakes, and the Coffee Cake stands up to any I've ever tasted. Finally, when you feel adventurous, please try to make the Bagels. There are quite a few steps, but they are rewarding!

May all your mornings have delicious beginnings.

Bagels

The really great thing about making gluten-free bagels is that you don't have to wait for the dough to rise. These bagels, like all bagels, require quite a bit of effort, but none of the steps is difficult.

For boiling water

1 teaspoon salt

Ingredients

1/3 cup lukewarm milk
1 packet yeast (about 1 tablespoon)
1 teaspoon sugar
1 egg
1/2 cup potato starch
3/4 cup cornstarch
1/4 teaspoon baking soda
1 teaspoon baking powder
1 teaspoon xanthan gum
1/2 teaspoon salt
1/4 teaspoon cider vinegar

For brushing on top of bagels

1 egg white, beaten

For baking sheet

1 tablespoon cornmeal (optional)

Directions

Preheat oven to 375°. Put a large pot of water on to boil. Add 1 teaspoon salt to water. In a large bowl, combine milk, yeast, and sugar. Stir well to dissolve yeast. Mix in egg. Add remaining ingredients. Mix well to remove all lumps.

Place dough on lightly "floured"—with cornstarch—surface. Divide into five disks. Using your thumbs, press a hole in middle of each dough disk. Shape into bagels.

Gently place bagels into boiling water. Boil for 30 seconds. Remove bagels from the water and place on a greased baking sheet or one sprinkled with cornmeal.

Brush with beaten egg white. Bake 15–18 minutes, until golden brown.

These bagels soften on standing but crisp well when toasted.

Makes 5 bagels.

Calories	157	Protein	3 g
Fat	1 g	Fiber	2 g
Cholesterol	44 mg	Sodium	631 mg
Carbohydrate	33 g		

Buttermilk Pancakes

These are mild, thick pancakes, fashioned after the buttermilk pancakes made from mixes that are found in the grocery store baking aisle. They are great served with butter and syrup.

Ingredients

1/4 cup sugar
2 tablespoons shortening
2 tablespoons oil
1 egg
3/4 cup cornstarch
3/4 cup potato starch
1/4 teaspoon xanthan gum
1/2 teaspoon salt
1 1/4 teaspoon baking powder
1/4 teaspoon baking soda
3/4 cup buttermilk

Directions

In medium mixing bowl, combine sugar and shortening. Mix well. Add all ingredients except buttermilk. While stirring, slowly add buttermilk, being sure to remove all lumps from the batter. Batter will be thin.

No buttermilk? Substitute 1 cup of milk plus 1 teaspoon vinegar for each 1 cup of buttermilk needed in a recipe.

Pour batter onto hot, greased griddle to make pancakes of the size you desire. I like to make 3-inch round pancakes. Turn pancakes over when they are lightly browned. When other side is lightly browned, remove from griddle and serve. Because these pancakes are thick, check the sides to be sure no damp batter shows. If it does, let them cook a bit longer.

Makes about 15 3-inch pancakes. Serves 3.

Calories	519	Protein	4 g
Fat	20 g	Fiber	1 g
Cholesterol	73 mg	Sodium	774 mg
Carbohydrate	81 g		

Cake Doughnuts

These doughnuts are just about all you'd want in a cake doughnut. They're not too heavy, not too sweet—a really nice taste. These doughnuts dry out quickly, so enjoy them right away. For longer-keeping doughnuts, try the Raised Doughnuts.

Ingredients

3/4 cup cornstarch
2/3 cup potato starch
1/3 cup sugar
1 tablespoon baking powder
1 egg
1/3 cup milk
1 teaspoon xanthan gum
1 teaspoon salt
2 tablespoons oil
1 teaspoon vanilla flavoring

For frying

2 cups vegetable oil

Topping

powdered sugar

Directions

Combine all ingredients in medium bowl. Mix well to remove all lumps.

Heat oil in medium saucepan to 375°. You may wish to use an electric fryer if you have one.

Pat out dough on "floured"—with cornstarch—surface to 1/3-inch thickness. Cut out doughnuts with round cookie cutter. Use apple corer or similar round object to remove center of doughnuts.

Place doughnuts and holes gently into hot oil; do not crowd them. Once they are lightly browned on both sides, remove and place on paper towels to drain.

Roll doughnuts (while still quite warm) in powdered sugar.

Makes about 9 doughnuts and 9 holes. Serve immediately. Serves 5.

Calories	376	Protein	2 g
Fat	20 g	Fiber	2 g
Cholesterol	44 mg	Sodium	769 mg
Carbohydrate	49 g		

Chipped Beef Gravy

There's a diner in the heart of Bethesda, Maryland, where my husband and I spent many mornings having breakfast. It was one of the few places that served chipped beef gravy, and they made it just right. This recipe is modeled after their fine presentation. I like this gravy over toast, but some people prefer biscuits. You choose.

Ingredients

1 3-ounce package chipped beef
2 tablespoons oil
1 1/2 cups milk (divided)
1 1/2 tablespoons cornstarch
pepper to taste (about 1/2 teaspoon)

Directions

Cut chipped beef into small pieces. Heat oil in a medium frying pan to medium heat. Add chipped beef. Cook until edges of beef curl up. Add 1 cup milk, stirring well.

Ingredient Alert—Watch for hidden gluten in the chipped beef. Brown sugar can contain colorings unacceptable to the gluten-free diet. Opt for a brand that uses regular sugar instead.

Combine remaining 1/2 cup milk and cornstarch in a cup. Mix well to dissolve. Add to beef. Stir well. Cook until thickened. Add pepper to taste. Salt is not needed.

Serve over biscuits or toast as desired. Makes 2 servings.

Calories	307	Protein	18 g
Fat	19 g	Fiber	0 g
Cholesterol	32 mg	Sodium	1550 mg
Carbohydrate	15 g		

Cinnamon-Raisin Biscuits

If you like biscuits in the morning, I'll bet you'll like these. They are light and flavorful.

Ingredients

1/3 cup shortening
1/2 cup potato starch
3/4 cup cornstarch
1 1/2 teaspoons xanthan gum
1 tablespoon baking powder
1/4 teaspoon baking soda
1/4 cup sugar
2/3 cup milk
1/2 teaspoon salt
3/4 teaspoon cinnamon
1/2 cup raisins
1/2 teaspoon vanilla flavoring

Directions

Preheat oven to 375°. In medium bowl, blend all ingredients. Mix very well to remove any lumps. Dough will be quite soft and a bit sticky.

Roll or pat out dough on a lightly "floured"—with cornstarch—surface. Dough should be about 1/2 inch thick. Cut out biscuits with 2 1/2-inch cookie cutter. An inverted glass will also do the job.

Place biscuits on lightly greased baking sheet. Bake 12–15 minutes, until lightly browned.

Makes 6–8 biscuits. Serves 6.

Calories	288	Protein	1 g
Fat	12 g	Fiber	3 g
Cholesterol	2 mg	Sodium	513 mg
Carbohydrate	45 g		

Coffee Cake

This delicious coffee cake is full of cinnamon flavor. It is soft and has a slight crumb.

Topping

1/2 teaspoon cinnamon
4 tablespoons sugar
2 tablespoons butter, softened

Ingredients

1 egg
1/4 cup oil
1/4 cup sugar
1/2 cup potato starch
3/4 cup cornstarch
1/4 teaspoon baking soda
1 1/2 teaspoons xanthan gum
1 tablespoon baking powder
2/3 cup milk
1/2 teaspoon salt
1 teaspoon vanilla flavoring
2 tablespoons shortening

Directions

Preheat oven to 350°. In small bowl, combine topping ingredients. Set aside.

In medium bowl, combine all other ingredients. Mix well, being sure to remove all lumps from batter. Pour batter into greased 8 × 8 baking pan.

Sprinkle topping over top of cake batter. Cut in topping as you would for a marble cake—holding knife point-down, make circular motions through batter.

Bake approximately 40 minutes, until toothpick inserted in middle tests clean.

Makes 9 servings. Freeze extra.

Calories	234	Protein	1 g
Fat	13 g	Fiber	1 g
Cholesterol	32 mg	Sodium	376 mg
Carbohydrate	29 g		

Danish

This Danish recipe is made with a light-airy bread dough molded with the back of a spoon.

Ingredients

2 tablespoons shortening
1/4 cup honey
1 egg
1 packet yeast (about 1 tablespoon)
1/2 cup sour cream
1/4 cup potato starch
3/4 cup cornstarch
1/4 teaspoon baking soda
1 teaspoon baking powder
1 teaspoon xanthan gum
1/2 teaspoon salt
1/2 teaspoon vinegar

For toppings

3 ounces cream cheese, room temperature
5 tablespoons powdered sugar
1 fresh peach, medium
2 teaspoons sugar
1 1/2 teaspoons cornstarch
1/4 cup water

Directions

Preheat oven to 350°. Combine all ingredients. Mix well to remove all lumps.

Place approximately 1/4 cup of dough in a small oval on greased baking sheet. Flatten to 1/4 inch. Repeat until all dough is used. Set aside.

A bit of your favorite jam is a delicious alternative to making the peach filling. Just use a tablespoon of jam on each danish.

In small bowl, combine cream cheese and powdered sugar. Blend well. Set aside.

In glass measuring cup, combine peeled and sliced peach, 2 teaspoons sugar, 1 1/2 teaspoons cornstarch, and 1/4 cup water. Mix well to fully dissolve cornstarch. Microwave on high for 1–3 minutes, until filling is translucent and thickened. Set aside.

Place a rounded spoonful of cream cheese mixture and a spoonful of peach mixture on top of each danish.

Bake approximately 15 minutes, until golden brown.

Makes 6 large danish.

Calories	297	Protein	3 g
Fat	13 g	Fiber	2 g
Cholesterol	57 mg	Sodium	383 mg
Carbohydrate	42 g		

French Toast

Any of this book's breads are nice for use in this French Toast, but you may substitute any gluten-free bread you like.

Ingredients

3 eggs
1/3 cup milk
1/2 teaspoon vanilla flavoring
1/4 teaspoon cinnamon
pinch of salt (optional)
6 slices of bread

Directions

In a flat-bottomed pie plate or bowl, mix all ingredients, except bread. Mix well, fully incorporating eggs.

Heat griddle or frying pan to medium temperature. Apply nonstick spray. The griddle or pan should not smoke.

Place piece of bread in batter for a moment, then turn it over to coat both sides well. Do not soak. Immediately place slice onto hot griddle or pan. Repeat for remaining slices. Turn slices when lightly browned. Once they are browned on both sides and cooked through, remove from griddle and serve.

Makes 6 slices. Serves 3.

Calories	270	Protein	8 g
Fat	14 g	Fiber	0 g
Cholesterol	215 mg	Sodium	97 mg
Carbohydrate	26 g		

Pancakes

Here is a thin, light, and tasty pancake. Nothing fancy—just basic pancakes.

Ingredients

- 1/4 cup oil
- 1/4 cup sugar
- 1 egg
- 3/4 cup cornstarch
- 3/4 cup potato starch
- 1/4 teaspoon guar gum
- 1/2 teaspoon salt
- 1 1/4 teaspoons baking powder
- 3/4 cup milk

Directions

In medium mixing bowl, combine all ingredients except milk. While stirring, slowly add milk, being sure to remove all lumps from the batter. Batter will be thin.

Pour batter onto hot, greased griddle to make pancakes of the size you desire. Turn pancakes over when lightly browned. When other side is lightly browned, remove from griddle and serve.

Makes about 12 4-inch pancakes. Serves 4.

Calories	399	Protein	3 g
Fat	16 g	Fiber	0 g
Cholesterol	57 mg	Sodium	476 mg
Carbohydrate	61 g		

Sausage Gravy

My good friend Cathy is a fine cook, though she usually spoils her guests with rich, delicious dishes. This gravy is no exception and really makes breakfast special. Enjoy this gravy over biscuits or toast.

Ingredients

8 ounces gluten-free sausage
1 1/2 cups milk (divided)
1 1/2 tablespoons cornstarch
salt to taste (about 1/2 teaspoon)
pepper to taste

Ingredient Alert—Sausage may contain gluten. It is important to know that your brand is gluten-free. At this writing, Jimmy Dean's fresh pork sausage does not contain gluten.

Directions

Fry sausage over medium heat in frying pan until well crumbled and cooked through. (You can drain the sausage if you like.) Add 1 cup milk, stirring well.

Combine remaining 1/2 cup milk and cornstarch in a cup. Mix well to dissolve. Add to sausage. Cook until thickened. Add salt and pepper to taste.

Serve over biscuits or toast as desired.

Makes 2 servings.

Calories	514	Protein	21 g
Fat	38 g	Fiber	0 g
Cholesterol	105 mg	Sodium	1540 mg
Carbohydrate	14 g		

Raised Doughnuts

These doughnuts are not raised at all. They are, however, as close to a raised doughnut as it gets. Close your eyes and take a taste. Except for the shape, you're not missing a thing. Oh, by the way, these doughnuts take minutes to make. Regular raised doughnuts take hours.

Ingredients

1/2 cup potato starch
1/2 cup cornstarch
2 tablespoons sugar
1/4 teaspoon baking soda
1 teaspoon baking powder
1 egg
scant 1/2 cup buttermilk
1/2 teaspoon xanthan gum
1/4 teaspoon vanilla flavoring
pinch of salt

For frying

2 cups vegetable oil

Glaze ingredients

1/2 cup powdered sugar
1/8 cup water

Directions

Combine all ingredients in medium bowl. Mix well to remove all lumps. Batter will thicken slightly; give it a minute or two.

Heat oil in medium saucepan to 375°. You may wish to use an electric fryer if you have one.

Drop batter by rounded teaspoon into hot oil. Do not crowd doughnuts.

Once lightly browned on both sides, remove and place on paper towels to drain.

To make glaze, combine powdered sugar and water. Stir until all lumps are dissolved. Dip doughnuts (while still quite warm) into glaze to coat. Allow to cool. Doughnuts may also be rolled in powdered sugar alone if desired.

Makes about 20 small doughnuts. Serves 5.

Calories	294	Protein	2 g
Fat	14 g	Fiber	1 g
Cholesterol	44 mg	Sodium	237 mg
Carbohydrate	41 g		

Sour Cream Breakfast Muffins

Do you like the taste of coffee cake, but really want individual servings? If so, this recipe is for you. These muffins are very soft and tender.

Ingredients

1/4 cup shortening
1/2 cup sugar
3/4 cup cornstarch
1/2 cup potato starch
1 cup sour cream
2 eggs
2 teaspoons baking powder
1/4 teaspoon baking soda
1/2 teaspoon salt
1/2 scant teaspoon xanthan gum

For topping

1/2 teaspoon cinnamon
2 tablespoons sugar

Directions

Preheat oven to 350°. In medium bowl, combine shortening and sugar. Mix well. Add remaining ingredients. Mix well to remove all lumps.

Combine sugar and cinnamon for topping. Set aside.

Fill greased muffin tins (or tins with paper liners) about 2/3 full. Sprinkle small amount of cinnamon-sugar on top of each muffin. Swirl the cinnamon-sugar into the muffin batter with the edge of a knife or back end of a spoon.

Bake 20–25 minutes, until toothpick inserted in muffin tests clean. Top of muffin should not look wet.

Makes 12–14 muffins. Serves 12.

Calories	174	Protein	2 g
Fat	9 g	Fiber	0 g
Cholesterol	42 mg	Sodium	223 mg
Carbohydrate	24 g		

Sourdough Pancakes

This is a pancake with a light sourdough taste. It is the preferred pancake in our home. These pancakes are easy to make; just remember to begin the starter the night before.

Starter

1/4 cup warm water
2 tablespoons sugar
1 packet yeast (about 1 tablespoon)
1/2 teaspoon salt

Ingredients

3 tablespoons oil
1 tablespoon shortening
2 tablespoons sugar
1 egg
3/4 cup cornstarch
3/4 cup potato starch
1/4 teaspoon xanthan gum
1 1/4 teaspoons baking powder
1/2 cup milk

Directions

In medium (nonmetal) bowl, combine all starter ingredients. Stir well. Let set at room temperature overnight.

In the same bowl, add all other ingredients except for milk. Stir well to remove all lumps. While stirring, slowly add milk, being sure no lumps remain.

Heat griddle or pan to medium heat. Apply nonstick spray to griddle. Griddle or pan should not smoke. Pour small amounts of batter onto hot griddle to make pancakes of the size you desire. Turn pancakes over when lightly browned. When both sides of pancakes are lightly browned, remove from griddle and serve.

Makes about 12 4-inch pancakes. Serves 4.

Calories	393	Protein	3 g
Fat	16 g	Fiber	1 g
Cholesterol	56 mg	Sodium	470 mg
Carbohydrate	61 g		

Special Waffles

This is my version of a Belgian waffle made in a regular waffle iron. They are my favorite waffle.

Ingredients

2 eggs, separated
2 tablespoons shortening
2 tablespoons oil
1/4 cup sugar
3/4 cup cornstarch
3/4 cup potato starch
1 1/2 teaspoons baking powder
1/4 teaspoon xanthan gum
1/2 teaspoon salt
1/2 teaspoon cinnamon
1/2 teaspoon vanilla flavoring
3/4 cup milk

Directions

In medium bowl, beat egg whites to stiff peaks. Set aside.

In another medium bowl, combine all ingredients, except for egg whites and milk. While mixing, slowly add milk, being sure to remove all lumps from the batter. Gently fold egg whites into batter.

Preheat waffle iron. Spray with nonstick spray. Pour about 2/3 cup of batter onto waffle iron. Once waffle is light brown, remove from waffle iron and serve.

Makes about 6 7-inch diameter round waffles. Serves 6.

Calories	276	Protein	3 g
Fat	11 g	Fiber	1 g
Cholesterol	73 mg	Sodium	350 mg
Carbohydrate	41 g		

Waffles

Here is a light, everyday waffle. Enjoy!

Ingredients

1/3 cup oil
1/4 cup sugar
2 eggs
3/4 cup cornstarch
3/4 cup potato starch
1 1/4 teaspoons baking powder
1/4 teaspoon xanthan gum
1/2 teaspoon salt
3/4 cup milk

Directions

In medium bowl, combine all ingredients except milk. While mixing, slowly add milk, being sure to remove all lumps from the batter.

Preheat waffle iron. Spray with nonstick spray. Pour about 2/3 cup of batter onto waffle iron. This will nearly cover the waffle dimples on the bottom of the iron. Once waffle is light brown, remove from waffle iron and serve.

Makes about 4 7-inch diameter round waffles. Serves 4.

Calories	458	Protein	5 g
Fat	22 g	Fiber	1 g
Cholesterol	110 mg	Sodium	492 mg
Carbohydrate	61 g		

Streusel Cake

This cake is really more of a pastry than a cake. On the bottom of this treat is a sweet bread dough. On top is Streusel, enhanced only by a bit of extra cinnamon.

Ingredients

2 tablespoons shortening
2 tablespoons honey
2 tablespoons sugar
1 egg
1 packet yeast (about 1 tablespoon)
1/2 cup sour cream
1/4 cup potato starch
3/4 cup cornstarch
1/4 teaspoon baking soda
3/4 teaspoon baking powder
1 teaspoon xanthan gum
1/2 teaspoon salt
1/2 teaspoon vinegar
1/2 teaspoon vanilla flavoring

For topping

Streusel (page 262), mixed but not baked, with cinnamon increased to 3/4 teaspoon.

Directions

Preheat oven to 350°. Combine all ingredients. Mix well to remove all lumps.

The dough will be quite wet. Place dough in base of 9 × 13 baking pan. The dough will be easier to manipulate with wet fingertips.

Here's a chance to get creative. One-half cup of jam can be used to enhance the streusel topping. Place small spoonfuls of your favorite jam on the cake before baking. Omit the extra cinnamon in the streusel if it does not compliment your jam choice.

Top with Streusel.

Bake approximately 25 minutes until lightly browned, and a toothpick inserted in the middle of the cake tests clean.

Makes 15 servings.

Calories	225	Protein	1 g
Fat	10 g	Fiber	2 g
Cholesterol	17 mg	Sodium	272 mg
Carbohydrate	33 g		

CHAPTER 3

Lunch and Dinner

When I first contemplated this chapter, I was certain that readers would prefer to make their own substitutions and changes in recipes. Then I realized that not only is this yet another chore in adjusting to dietary restrictions but that also some of you may still be learning which foods and ingredients are safe.

As with the other chapters, I have used the most basic ingredients possible so that your meals will come together without hesitation. Hopefully, this chapter will help you modify your cooking style by substituting safe, readily available ingredients instead of seeking out expensive specialty substitutes.

Eating gluten-free does not necessitate special servings for one. It can be a crowd-pleasing affair with a big pot of Chili, an intimate dinner for two with Seafood Crepes, or a family meal with Marinated Grilled Chicken. Please share these delicious entrees with the special people in your life.

Chicken Rice Soup

Here is the favorite soup in our home. I hope it becomes one of your favorites, too.

Ingredients

1 frying chicken, 2 1/2–3 pounds (or similar weight of pieces)
1 onion, unpeeled and cut in quarters
2/3 cup rice (short-grain preferred)
1 medium onion, chopped fine
2 1/2 teaspoons salt
1 teaspoon pepper

Directions

In large pot, combine freshly washed chicken and onion. Cover with water and cook until very tender, 60–90 minutes. Remove chicken and onion from broth.

You should have approximately 10–11 cups of broth. Add water to equal that amount or continue to simmer broth to reduce to that amount of broth.

Remove chicken from bones and return chicken pieces to broth. To broth, add remaining ingredients, and cook uncovered until rice is tender.

Serves 12.

Calories	104	Protein	10 g
Fat	2 g	Fiber	1 g
Cholesterol	27 mg	Sodium	473 mg
Carbohydrate	10 g		

Chicken Breast with Wine and Mushrooms

Here is a very nice quick entrée. It takes less than 30 minutes from beginning to table. I like to use a dry white wine, but you should substitute your preference. If you don't care to drink wine, consider purchasing a single-serving bottle instead of a regular bottle to limit waste.

Ingredients

4	tablespoons butter, divided
4	boneless chicken breast halves
4–5	large mushrooms, sliced
1/2	cup white wine
3/4	teaspoon salt
1/2	teaspoon pepper
1/2	cup water
2	teaspoons cornstarch

Directions

In large frying pan, melt 2 tablespoons butter and fry chicken breasts until cooked through. Chicken will cook more quickly if covered, in about 20 minutes. No pink should remain. Remove chicken from pan and set aside.

To pan, add remaining 2 tablespoons butter and mushrooms. Cook until mushrooms are tender. Scrape bottom of pan to incorporate any food particles on the bottom of pan. Add wine, salt, and pepper and stir well.

Combine water and cornstarch. Add slowly to wine in saucepan. Cook until sauce is thickened.

Return chicken to pan until serving. Serve sauce over top of chicken.

Serves 4.

Calories	332	Protein	30 g
Fat	20 g	Fiber	0 g
Cholesterol	115 mg	Sodium	597 mg
Carbohydrate	3 g		

Chicken Pot Pie

Sometimes the safest meals are made from scratch. This recipe is not difficult, so please give yourself a chance to enjoy this home-made favorite.

Recommended crust

Traditional Piecrust (prepared but not baked), (page 232)

For filling

2 1/2–3	pounds chicken pieces
1	medium onion, with peel on, cut into 4 pieces
1	bay leaf (optional)
1	large potato, peeled and diced
1 1/2	cups frozen, mixed vegetables
1	small onion, peeled, chopped
	salt to taste (1 teaspoon)
	pepper to taste (1/2 teaspoon)
3	tablespoons cornstarch
1/4	cup water

In this recipe, it is desirable to use a white or red potato. Avoid a mealy potato, like russet, as it may impart a starchy flavor in this use.

Directions

Prepare piecrust dough; set aside.

Preheat oven to 375°.

Place chicken, onion, and bay leaf in large pot with 10 cups water. Bring to a boil. Cover and cook until tender, approximately 1 1/2 hours.

Remove chicken, onion, and bay leaf from broth. Remove chicken from the bone; cut into bite-size pieces. Discard cooked onion and bay leaf.

To broth, add potato, frozen mixed vegetables, and onion. Cook until potato and vegetables are tender. Drain broth into separate pan. Boil broth uncovered until it is reduced to about 1 1/2 cups. To broth add salt and pepper to taste. Combine cornstarch with 1/4 cup water. Add to boiling broth. Stir until thickened.

Place chicken and vegetables in thickened broth. Mix well to coat. Pour into 1 1/2 quart casserole (or a pie pan).

Roll out piecrust between two sheets of waxed paper to shape of casserole dish. Place crust on top of casserole. Cut a few slits on top to vent. If casserole dish is very full, place baking sheet under casserole to catch any overflows in the oven.

Bake 20–25 minutes, until crust is nicely browned.

Serves 6.

Calories	457	Protein	20 g
Fat	22 g	Fiber	7 g
Cholesterol	55 mg	Sodium	616 mg
Carbohydrate	44 g		

Chili

This recipe will make you forget any mix you've used before. Using red bell pepper and black beans makes for a more refined flavor than the usual kidney beans and green bell pepper. I like my food spicy, as is this Chili. Should you prefer your foods milder, cut back the ground red pepper and black pepper by half.

Ingredients

1 medium onion, chopped
1 red bell pepper, chopped
3 pounds of ground chuck
2 cups water
2 16-ounce cans black beans
2 6-ounce cans tomato paste
3 teaspoons salt
1 teaspoon black pepper
1 teaspoon ground red pepper
1 teaspoon cumin
1 teaspoon oregano
1 clove garlic, minced

Directions

In large pot, combine onion, bell pepper, and ground chuck. Cook over medium heat until cooked through and no longer pink.

To cooked meat mixture, add remaining ingredients and mix well. Simmer over low heat at least 30 minutes to allow the flavors to blend.

Makes 12 servings.

Calories	272	Protein	28 g
Fat	9 g	Fiber	6 g
Cholesterol	74 mg	Sodium	838 mg
Carbohydrate	20 g		

Fried Chicken

Fried chicken is definitely not a first choice for low-fat cooking, but it sure does taste good. This coating is not too heavy and not too light—just right.

Ingredients

1 frying chicken, 2 1/2–3 pounds
1/2 cup cornstarch
1/2 cup potato starch
1 teaspoon salt
1 teaspoon pepper
1/2 teaspoon xanthan gum
1/2 teaspoon baking soda
1/2 teaspoon ground red pepper (optional)

For frying

2 cups oil

Directions

Cut chicken into desired pieces. Rinse and set aside.

Place remaining ingredients into large freezer bag or paper lunch bag. Shake to mix well.

Heat oil in frying pan to 375°.

One at a time, place chicken pieces in bag and coat well with flour mixture. Press flour mixture firmly onto chicken if needed.

Place coated chicken into frying pan. Repeat for remaining pieces of chicken. Fry on each side for approximately 15 minutes. No pink should be seen in the meat; or, if you have a meat thermometer, the chicken should reach a temperature of 185°.

Alternatively, chicken may be deep fried for approximately 20 minutes.

Makes 8 pieces of chicken. Serves 4.

Calories	558	Protein	32 g
Fat	33 g	Fiber	1 g
Cholesterol	153 mg	Sodium	814 mg
Carbohydrate	31 g		

Ham and Cheese Pocket Pies

Here's a tasty on-the-go dinner. It is a bit of a fuss to manipulate the piecrust the first time you prepare this dish, but soon you'll master its assembly.

Recommended crust

Traditional Piecrust (prepared but not baked), (page 232)

For filling

- 1/2 cup finely chopped cooked ham
- 1/2 cup grated cheddar cheese
- 1/2 cup finely chopped broccoli or onion

Directions

Prepare piecrust dough; set aside.

Preheat oven to 375°. For filling, combine all ingredients in small bowl. Set aside.

Roll out 1/2 of dough between two sheets of waxed paper. Remove top piece of waxed paper; turn waxed paper over. Recover dough with waxed paper and flip dough over. (This will make handling of dough easier in later step.) Remove new top layer of waxed paper. Cut dough into two large rectangles. Place approximately 1/4–1/3 cup of filling to one side of rectangle. While leaving waxed paper on the downside of the dough, fold dough in half over filling to form a square. Slowly remove waxed paper and press edges of dough together to seal.

Place pies on greased baking sheet. Prick tops of pies a few times to allow steam to escape. Repeat rolling and filling until all dough is used. Bake 20–25 minutes, until pies are browned and cheese is melted.

Makes 4 pies. Serves 4.

Calories	487	Protein	8 g
Fat	32 g	Fiber	7 g
Cholesterol	25 mg	Sodium	592 mg
Carbohydrate	42 g		

Marinated Grilled Chicken

This recipe may be baked if desired. It has a very mild, almost fragrant, flavor.

Ingredients

8 ounces plain yogurt
1/4 cup lemon juice
1 tablespoon dried rosemary
1/2 teaspoon salt
2 1/2 pounds chicken pieces

Directions

Combine all ingredients except chicken in large bowl. Mix well. Add chicken pieces and coat well with marinade. Refrigerate overnight (or at least 4 hours).

Prepare barbecue grill. Place chicken over hot coals and cook until no pink remains. Depending on the grill, this will be between 45 and 60 minutes.

Alternatively, preheat oven to 400°. Place chicken on greased baking sheet. Bake 50–60 minutes, until no pink remains. If you have a meat thermometer, the chicken should reach 185°.

Serves 6.

Calories	255	Protein	22 g
Fat	17 g	Fiber	0 g
Cholesterol	103 mg	Sodium	132 mg
Carbohydrate	1 g		

Meat Loaf

This is family-style meat loaf, plain and simple. No flavor has been lost in modifying this recipe, and no shopping for special ingredients was needed.

Ingredients

2 pounds ground chuck
1 onion, chopped
1 egg
2 tablespoons tomato paste
1 1/2 teaspoons salt
1 teaspoon pepper
1 small potato, unpeeled and grated

Directions

Preheat oven to 375°.

In large bowl, combine all ingredients and mix well. Place mixture in 9 × 4 loaf pan. Bake 1 hour and 20 minutes, until cooked through. If you have a meat thermometer, meat loaf should reach temperature of 160°.

Serves 8.

Calories	331	Protein	22 g
Fat	24 g	Fiber	1 g
Cholesterol	112 mg	Sodium	410 mg
Carbohydrate	6 g		

Onion Rings

Aren't onion rings wonderful? This version is crisp with a light batter coating.

Ingredients

1 large onion, peeled and cut into thick slices
1/2 cup cornstarch
1/2 cup potato starch
1/2 teaspoon salt
1/2 teaspoon baking powder
1/4 teaspoon baking soda
scant 1/2 teaspoon xanthan gum
pinch of ground red pepper (optional)
3/4 cup milk

For frying

2 cups oil

Directions

Separate onion slices into individual rings. Set aside.

In small bowl, combine all other ingredients. Mix well to form a smooth batter. Allow batter to sit for a few minutes. It will thicken a little and adhere better to the onion rings.

Heat oil in small saucepan to 375°.

Dip onion slices into batter and place into hot oil. Do not crowd. Cook until lightly browned. Drain on paper towels. Sprinkle with additional salt as desired.

Serves 2.

Calories	599	Protein	5 g
Fat	30 g	Fiber	5 g
Cholesterol	7 mg	Sodium	880 mg
Carbohydrate	79 g		

Roast Beef with Gravy

This is one of my favorite dishes and very easy to prepare. Grab the crock pot for this delicious recipe. I've used chuck roast to assure lots of broth for the gravy.

Ingredients

1 boneless chuck roast, about 2 pounds
1/2 cup water
2 1/2 tablespoons cornstarch
3/4 teaspoon salt
1/2 teaspoon pepper

Directions

Place roast in crock pot. Add nothing at this time. Turn on high for 1/2 day or on low for full day. Roast will be very tender. Drain broth into small saucepan. The broth should approximate 1 1/2 cups. If less, add water to make 1 1/2 cups. If more, simmer broth to reduce to approximately 1 1/2 cups.

In saucepan, bring broth to boil. Add salt and pepper. Combine water and cornstarch. Add to broth while stirring. Bring to boil again to thicken.

Serves 4.

Calories	357	Protein	44 g
Fat	17 g	Fiber	0 g
Cholesterol	147 mg	Sodium	575 mg
Carbohydrate	5 g		

Pork Scallopini

This quick entrée is delicious. I've used pork instead of the traditional veal to make it more affordable.

Ingredients

4 boneless pork chops
2 tablespoons cornstarch
2 tablespoons potato starch
pinch of salt
pinch of pepper
2 tablespoons butter
1/2 cup white wine
3/4 teaspoon salt
1/2 teaspoon pepper
1 cup water
2 tablespoons cornstarch

Directions

Pound pork chops very thin, about 1/4 inch. If you do not have a meat mallet, a wooden rolling pin works well.

On a plate, combine 2 tablespoons cornstarch, 2 tablespoons potato starch, pinch of salt, and pinch of pepper. Coat each chop with this flour mixture.

In large pan, melt butter. Pan-fry each chop until cooked through. Remove from pan and set aside.

To pan, add wine, 3/4 teaspoon salt, and 1/2 teaspoon pepper. Scrape the bottom of the pan to incorporate any food particles on the bottom of the pan. Combine water and cornstarch. Add to pan, stirring well. Allow sauce to cook for a few minutes, so flavors mingle.

Serve sauce over chops. Serves 4.

Calories	323	Protein	31 g
Fat	14 g	Fiber	0 g
Cholesterol	97 mg	Sodium	565 mg
Carbohydrate	12 g		

Pizza

This recipe is for those of you who have never made a homemade pizza before. I have used the plainest, safest ingredients possible. This pizza is fun to make with the kids.

Recommended crust

Pizza Crust (freshly made but not baked),
(page 102)

For topping

1 6-ounce can tomato paste
2–3 tablespoons water
1 clove garlic, crushed and finely chopped
1 tablespoon fresh oregano or 3/4 teaspoon dried oregano
1/4 teaspoon salt
1/8 teaspoon pepper
1 1/2 cups grated mozzarella cheese
2 tablespoons parmesan cheese, grated

Optional toppings

1 small onion, peeled and sliced
3 large mushrooms, sliced
4 ounces sausage, crumbled, fried, and drained

Directions

Prepare Pizza Crust. Press out on greased baking sheet to 12-inch circle. Set aside.

Preheat oven to 400°.

In small bowl, combine tomato paste, water, and garlic. Blend well. Pour desired amount of this sauce over top of dough, and spread it with your fingers or the back of a spoon.

Ingredient Alert—Did you know that some tomato pastes contain ingredients other than tomatoes? And the same applies to tomato sauce. It is best to be cautious of ingredients of unknown origin.

Sprinkle oregano, garlic, salt, and pepper over top of sauce. Then spread cheeses on top of everything. Add any optional toppings you like.

Bake 20–25 minutes, until dough is lightly browned and crust is cooked through. The time varies depending on the thickness of the crust and the number of toppings. It is good to cut into the center of the pizza to check for doneness or to lift the crust so that you can see how well cooked the crust is toward the center of the pizza.

Remove from oven. Cut into 6 slices.

Serves 3.

Calories	608	Protein	20 g
Fat	29 g	Fiber	11 g
Cholesterol	39 mg	Sodium	1212 mg
Carbohydrate	69 g		

Quiche

If you like smooth custard-like Quiche Lorraine, this may not be the quiche for you. If you like real, substantial food, you'll like this quiche. It is flavorful and perfect with a salad or fruit for a special meal.

Recommended crust

Traditional Pie Crust (prepared but not baked), (page 232)

For filling

1 small onion, chopped
1 tablespoon oil
1 cup chopped ham, cooked
2 cups grated cheddar cheese
4 eggs
3/4 cup milk
1/4 teaspoon salt (omit if using country ham)
1/4 teaspoon pepper

Directions

Prepare piecrust. Set aside.

Preheat oven to 400°.

In small greased skillet, fry onion in oil until softened. Pour onion into piecrust. Put ham and cheddar cheese in piecrust as well.

This Quiche is even better if you use a good country ham in place of regular ham. After cooking the country ham (slices), rinse them with water to cut the salt level.

In medium bowl, combine eggs, milk, salt, and pepper. Mix well. Pour egg mixture over ingredients already in piecrust.

Bake 10 minutes. Turn heat down to 325°. Bake an additional 25–30 minutes, until eggs are fully set. A knife inserted in middle will test clean.

Serves 6.

Calories	552	Protein	20 g
Fat	38 g	Fiber	5 g
Cholesterol	196 mg	Sodium	854 mg
Carbohydrate	33 g		

Stuffing

Does anyone know why stuffing is made using dried-out bread cubes, when it's all going to be moistened again anyway? Surely using broth to bring back the moisture and heighten the flavor of the stuffing can't be worth it. Frankly, I don't see gluten-free breads having a fighting chance of being dried out and then moistened again (they'd just fall apart). So I don't do it. Now, if you happen to have extra pieces of stale bread, you can use them, but increase the liquid in this recipe a little.

Ingredients

5–7 slices gluten-free bread, torn into small pieces
1 small onion, finely chopped
1 teaspoon dried sage
1 egg
salt and pepper to taste (more than you'd think)
up to 1/2 cup water or broth

Directions

In medium bowl, place all ingredients except liquid. Toss well. Do not smash the bread. Add a small amount of water or broth to moisten the bread mixture. Stuffing should feel like a damp sponge. Again, toss to combine; do not smash bread.

Place stuffing inside cavity of cleaned chicken or into greased baking dish. A small casserole is ideal.

If baking alone, bake at 375° for 35 minutes, until top is lightly browned and stuffing is hot throughout.

Makes approximately 3 cups stuffing. Serves 4.

Calories	152	Protein	3 g
Fat	6 g	Fiber	1 g
Cholesterol	53 mg	Sodium	31 mg
Carbohydrate	19 g		

Beef Vegetable Soup

Homemade soup is a favorite in our home. This recipe makes a big pot of soup, and it freezes well.

Ingredients

2–2 1/2	pounds boneless chuck roast
1	unpeeled onion, cut in quarters
1	bay leaf, optional
1/2	cup tomato paste
2	pounds frozen mixed vegetables
2	medium potatoes, unpeeled and diced
1	small onion, chopped
2 1/2	teaspoons salt
1	teaspoon pepper

Directions

In large pot, place roast, onion, and bay leaf. Cover with water. Cook covered over medium heat until meat is very tender, 2–3 hours. Remove meat from broth. Discard onion and bay leaf.

Measure broth. Add water to make 6 cups. If you have more broth than 6 cups, simmer uncovered until broth is reduced to about that amount.

To broth, add tomato paste, frozen vegetables, potatoes, chopped onion, salt, and pepper. While vegetables are cooking, remove fat from meat and cut/tear into small pieces and return to broth. Allow soup to simmer for at least 30 minutes, so flavors mingle.

Serves 12.

Calories	210	Protein	18 g
Fat	6 g	Fiber	5 g
Cholesterol	49 mg	Sodium	542 mg
Carbohydrate	22 g		

Seafood Crepes

This recipe uses scallops and shrimp to make a terrific upscale dinner, but you may substitute other seafood. Share this meal with someone special.

Recommended wrappers

1 recipe Crepes (page 256), freshly prepared without vanilla flavoring

Ingredients

4 tablespoons butter
1/4 pound of bay scallops (the small ones)
1/4 pound shrimp, peeled and deveined
1 tablespoon lemon juice
pinch of salt (less than you'd think)
pinch of pepper

My girlfriend Shaunna taught me the easiest way to devein a shrimp. Place a toothpick through the back of the shrimp, just below the vein. Then pull the toothpick through the back and the vein will be removed.

Directions

Prepare crepes as directed. Cover to keep warm.

In small saucepan, heat butter until melted. Add scallops and shrimp. Cook until shrimp are pink and scallops are white. (The shrimp and scallops should not appear translucent.) Add lemon juice, salt, and pepper.

Remove from heat. Spoon small amounts shrimp and scallops into middle of each crepe. Fold sides over top of filling. Place on serving plate. Spoon small amount of lemon-butter from pan over top. Garnish with lemon slices.

Makes 5–6 crepes. Serves 2.

Calories	483	Protein	31 g
Fat	34 g	Fiber	0 g
Cholesterol	492 mg	Sodium	630 mg
Carbohydrate	12 g		

Shepherd's Pie

Here is a dinner pie that you may have first enjoyed at a grandparent's home. I've seen a few versions, but they always use convenience products. As with most foods, though, this is better prepared from scratch.

Recommended crust

Traditional Piecrust (prepared, baked, and cooled), (page 232)

Ingredients for mashed potatos layer

4–5 large potatoes (russet preferred)
2 tablespoons butter (optional)
1/4 teaspoon salt
3/4 cup milk, more or less

For meat filling

1 medium onion, chopped
1 1/4 pounds lean ground beef or ground chuck
1 teaspoon salt
1/2 teaspoon pepper
1 cup frozen peas and carrots or 1 cup fresh squash, diced
1 1/4 cups water or milk, divided
2 tablespoons cornstarch

Directions

Prepare piecrust. Bake and cool.

Peel and dice potatoes. Place in medium pot of water. Cook until tender. Drain. Add butter, salt, and enough milk to whip potatoes until light and moist. Set aside. Preheat oven to 375°.

In medium saucepan, fry onion and ground beef until well cooked. Add salt, pepper, vegetables, and 1 cup water or milk. Bring to boil. Combine 1/4 cup water or milk and cornstarch. Add to ground beef mixture and cook until thickened. Pour beef mixture into piecrust.

Top beef mixture with mashed potatoes. Bake approximately 25 minutes, until potatoes are lightly browned.

Makes 6 ample servings.

Calories	666	Protein	21 g
Fat	38 g	Fiber	10 g
Cholesterol	74 mg	Sodium	744 mg
Carbohydrate	60 g		

CHAPTER 4

Breads

Let me be up-front about gluten-free breads. They will never exactly duplicate wheat flavor. They are frequently mild in flavor yet certainly pleasant, much like a heavier white bread. If you find the basic loaves are too subtle for your tastebuds, I encourage you to try those loaves with something special about them—from Cottage Dill Loaf to Cheese Straws.

Despite their mild nature, please know that these plain loaves make the most wonderful toast I have ever eaten. It would be a shame to miss out on them. If you really want a very-near wheat taste, please try the Bread Sticks or Rolls first. It is hard to eat just one of these. They are two stars in this chapter. My favorite plain loaf of bread is the Buttermilk Loaf. I'm betting it will be a favorite of yours, too.

These breads are a snap to make—no kneading required. Most recipes are oven-ready in less than 5 minutes. Nice, hot bread from the oven in under an hour—wheat has nothing on us. Only the Sourdough Loaf takes longer to make because it is allowed to rise for a while so that its sourdough flavor can develop.

Some of you may be accustomed to using a bread machine. Because most of the loaves in this book need only

25–30 minutes of baking time, the machines are a bit brutal. (Yes, bread machines are very nice for "rice"-type breads, but not for these recipes.) And besides, a loaf out of the oven is usually much prettier than out of the bread machine.

Do you need to avoid yeast? If so, please know that yeast may be omitted from all but the sourdough recipes in this book. Other leavening, not the yeast, is responsible for most of the "rise" in these recipes. Yeast is used primarily for flavor.

Biscuits

This dough is quite soft, and so are the biscuits. Delicious.

Ingredients

1/3 cup shortening
1/2 cup potato starch
3/4 cup cornstarch
1 3/4 teaspoons xanthan gum
1 tablespoon baking powder
1/4 teaspoon baking soda
1 tablespoon sugar
3/4 cup milk
1/2 teaspoon salt

Directions

Preheat oven to 375°. In medium bowl, blend all ingredients. Mix very well to remove any lumps. Dough will be quite soft and a bit sticky.

Roll or pat out dough on a lightly "floured"—with cornstarch—surface. Dough should be about 1/2 inch thick. Cut out biscuits with 2 1/2 inch cookie cutters. An inverted glass will also do the job. Place biscuits on lightly greased baking sheet.

Bake 12–15 minutes, until lightly browned.

Makes 6–8 large biscuits. Serves 6.

Calories	230	Protein	1 g
Fat	12 g	Fiber	2 g
Cholesterol	2 mg	Sodium	513 mg
Carbohydrate	30 g		

All-Purpose Loaf

No kneading, no fuss, just a quick everyday loaf of bread. This loaf is comparable to a heavier white bread—plain but pleasant.

Ingredients

1 1/4 cups milk, room temperature
1 packet yeast (about 1 tablespoon)
1 1/4 cups potato starch
1 1/4 cups cornstarch
1 teaspoon salt
1 tablespoon baking powder
2 teaspoons xanthan gum
2 tablespoons honey
1/4 cup oil

Directions

Preheat oven to 350°. In small bowl, combine milk and yeast. Stir to dissolve yeast. Set aside.

In medium bowl, combine all dry ingredients. To dry ingredients, slowly add honey, oil, and milk/yeast mixture. Mix well. Dough will look wet, thick, and pasty.

Place dough into greased 9 × 4 loaf pan. Wet hands and smooth out top of dough, then press an indentation along the center lengthwise of the loaf. This will provide for a prettier loaf.

Bake 25–28 minutes. Loaf will just begin to brown. Test for doneness with a long toothpick, much as you would for a cake. Cool briefly before removing from pan. Refrigerate or freeze extra servings.

Makes 1 large loaf. Serves 10.

Calories	206	Protein	1 g
Fat	6 g	Fiber	2 g
Cholesterol	2 mg	Sodium	392 mg
Carbohydrate	36 g		

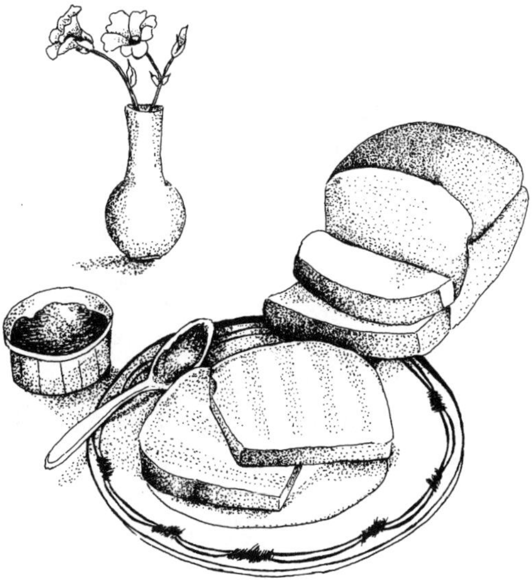

Buttermilk Loaf

This loaf has a nice, tight texture. It is quite soft yet has real bread structure. It is my favorite loaf of bread.

Ingredients

1 1/4 cups buttermilk, room temperature
1 packet yeast (about 1 tablespoon)
3/4 cup potato starch
1 1/4 cups cornstarch
2 tablespoons sugar
1/2 teaspoon baking soda
2 teaspoons baking powder
2 1/2 teaspoons xanthan gum
1/2 teaspoon salt
1/4 cup oil

Directions

Preheat oven to 350°. In a small bowl, combine buttermilk and yeast. Stir to dissolve yeast. Set aside.

In medium bowl, combine all dry ingredients. To dry ingredients, slowly add oil and milk/yeast mixture. Mix well. Dough will look wet, thick, and pasty.

Place dough into greased 9 × 4 loaf pan. Wet hands and smooth out top of dough, then make an indentation down the center lengthwise of loaf. This will make the loaf more attractive.

Bake 25–28 minutes. Loaf will just begin to brown. Test for doneness with a long toothpick, much as you would for a cake. Cool briefly before removing from pan. Refrigerate or freeze extra servings.

Makes 1 large loaf. Serves 10.

Calories	172	**Protein**	1 g
Fat	6 g	**Fiber**	2 g
Cholesterol	1 mg	**Sodium**	311 mg
Carbohydrate	29 g		

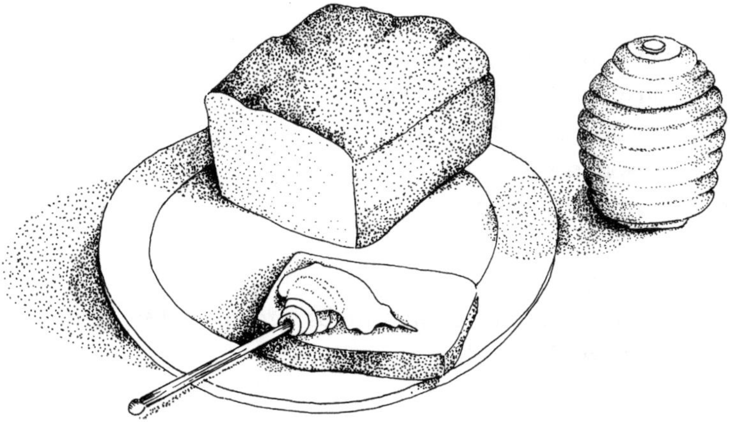

Bread Sticks

These bread sticks are light and airy, and the dough is not rolled out—it is piped from a pastry bag (or from the snipped-off corner of a plastic sandwich bag). You should know that I'll use any method at my disposal if it means the finished product will be more like its wheat-containing counterpart. These bread sticks are really delicious.

Ingredients

1/4 cup shortening
3 tablespoons honey
2 eggs
1 packet yeast (about 1 tablespoon)
1 cup unflavored yogurt
1/2 cup potato starch
1 1/2 cups cornstarch
1/2 teaspoon baking soda
2 teaspoons baking powder
2 teaspoons xanthan gum
3/4 teaspoon salt
3/4 teaspoon vinegar

For topping

Kosher salt and/or other herbs, grated cheese, sesame seeds, and so forth

My favorite all-purpose spice combination is Jane's Krazy Mixed-Up Salt. It is the perfect spice to top these bread sticks and confirmed gluten-free at the time of this writing.

Directions

Preheat oven to 350°. Combine all ingredients. Mix well to remove all lumps.

The dough will be quite wet. Place dough in a pastry bag with a large round tip (or use a plastic lunch bag with a bit of a corner cut off). Pipe dough into long strips (5–6 inches is nice) on greased baking sheet. Sprinkle with kosher salt and/or other toppings as desired.

Bake 10–12 minutes, until golden brown.

Makes 20–30 bread sticks. Serves 10.

Calories	196	Protein	3 g
Fat	7 g	Fiber	2 g
Cholesterol	44 mg	Sodium	361 mg
Carbohydrate	32 g		

Cheese Straws

These Cheese Straws are very cheesy and almost pastrylike. I personally like the bite of the red pepper, but if you prefer a milder taste, omit it. Use a crinkled-edge cutter to dress up these treats.

Ingredients

4 ounces cheddar cheese, very finely grated
1/4 cup softened butter
1/3 cup potato starch
1/2 cup cornstarch
pinch of salt
1/4 teaspoon ground red pepper (optional)
1/4 teaspoon xanthan gum
3 tablespoons cream

Ingredient Alert—Most, if not all, yellow-colored cheddar cheese contains annatto. It is not well-tolerated by some gluten-free individuals. Please opt for white cheddar cheese.

Directions

Preheat oven to 375°. Very finely grate cheddar cheese. Set aside.

Combine butter, potato starch, cornstarch, salt, red pepper, and xanthan gum. Mix well. Mixture will be quite crumbly. Add cream and beat until no lumps remain. Add cheese and mix well. Dough will be almost uniform in color.

Pat or roll out dough on unfloured surface to 1/4-inch thickness. The dough should not be sticky at this point. If it is sticky, refrigerate it for a few minutes. Cut straws approximately 1/3 inch wide and up to 5 inches long. Place on greased baking sheet.

Bake approximately 12 minutes.

Makes approximately 24 5-inch long cheese straws. Serves 6.

Calories	242	Protein	5 g
Fat	17 g	Fiber	0 g
Cholesterol	52 mg	Sodium	226 mg
Carbohydrate	17 g		

Cinnamon Loaf

When you first put together this "layered" loaf, it will seem like there is too much cinnamon/sugar mixture. There is not. This loaf expands a lot compared to its size when first put in the pan. It's a nice, not-too-sweet treat.

Ingredients

1 packet yeast (about 1 tablespoon)
1 1/4 cups milk, room temperature
1 1/4 teaspoons vinegar
3/4 cup potato starch
1 1/4 cups cornstarch
2 tablespoons sugar
1/2 teaspoon baking soda
2 teaspoons baking powder
2 1/2 teaspoons xanthan gum
1/2 teaspoon salt
1/4 cup oil

For filling

2 teaspoons cinnamon
1/4 cup sugar

Directions

Preheat oven to 350°. In small bowl, combine yeast, milk, and vinegar. Stir to dissolve yeast. Set aside.

In medium bowl, combine all dry ingredients. To dry ingredients, slowly add oil and milk/yeast/vinegar mixture. Mix well. Dough will look wet, thick, and pasty. Set aside.

Combine sugar and cinnamon; set aside.

Place approximately 1/3 of dough in greased 9 × 4 loaf pan; sprinkle with 1/3 of cinnamon/sugar mixture. Continue layering until all dough and a bit of cinnamon/sugar mixture remains for the top of the loaf.

Wet hands and smooth out top of dough, then press an indentation along center lengthwise of loaf. This will provide for a prettier loaf. Top with remaining cinnamon/sugar mixture.

Bake 25–28 minutes. Loaf will just begin to brown. Test for doneness with a long toothpick, much as you would for a cake. Cool briefly before removing from pan. Refrigerate or freeze extra servings.

Makes 1 large loaf. Serves 10.

Calories	194	Protein	1 g
Fat	6 g	Fiber	3 g
Cholesterol	2 mg	Sodium	294 mg
Carbohydrate	34 g		

Cinnamon Rolls

These cinnamon rolls will not quite make you forget those you used to buy at the mall, but these are nice. Please follow the unusual techniques carefully when you make these rolls. Enjoy!

Ingredients

2 tablespoons shortening
1/4 cup sugar
2/3 cup milk, room temperature
1 packet yeast (about 1 tablespoon)
1 egg
1/4 cup oil
1/2 cup potato starch
1 cup cornstarch
1/4 teaspoon baking soda
2 1/2 teaspoons xanthan gum
2 teaspoons baking powder
1/2 teaspoon salt
1 teaspoon vanilla flavoring

For tabletop

1–2 tablespoons sugar

For filling

1 cup brown sugar
1 1/4 teaspoons cinnamon

For glaze (optional)

3/4 cup powdered sugar
1 1/2 tablespoons milk
few drops of vanilla flavoring

Directions

Preheat oven to 375°. In medium bowl, combine shortening and sugar. Mix well. Measure milk and add yeast to milk. Mix well to fully dissolve. Add milk/yeast to sugar mixture. Add remaining ingredients. Mix very well, being sure to remove all lumps. Dough will be quite soft.

Sprinkle sugar on tabletop. Place dough on top of sugared area. Pat and/or roll dough out to $13\frac{1}{2} \times 13\frac{1}{2}$ inch square. Because this dough is very moist, you may wish to keep your hands damp with water or use a wet rolling pin to smooth out the dough.

Combine brown sugar and cinnamon. Spread evenly across dough's surface. Roll up dough to form a long cylinder. The edge of a ruler or spatula is helpful to roll the dough as it may stick a bit. The dough will again seem too wet for this use, but the moist dough ensures a moist roll. Cut into 9 slices of similar size (about $1\frac{1}{2}$ inches wide).

Place rolls into a greased 9 × 9 pan. Bake approximately 20 minutes, until tops are lightly browned.

Combine powdered sugar, milk, and vanilla flavoring to make glaze. Stir until all lumps are dissolved. Drizzle over warm rolls if desired.

Makes 9 modestly sized rolls. Serves 9.

Calories	308	Protein	2 g
Fat	10 g	Fiber	3 g
Cholesterol	25 mg	Sodium	301 mg
Carbohydrate	54 g		

Cornbread—Version 1

This cornbread is a lot like the one you mix up in just a few minutes from a box purchased at the grocery store. It really is terrific hot from the oven.

Ingredients

1 cup milk
1 egg
1/4 cup oil
1/4 teaspoon vinegar
1/3 cup potato starch
1/2 cup cornstarch
1 teaspoon salt
1/4 teaspoon baking soda
1 tablespoon baking powder
3/4 cup cornmeal
1/2 cup sugar
1/2 teaspoon xanthan gum

Directions

Preheat oven to 375°. In medium bowl, combine milk, egg, oil, and vinegar. Mix well. Add all other ingredients and mix well, being sure to remove any lumps. Batter will be thin.

Pour batter into greased 8 × 8 baking pan. Bake 28–32 minutes, until cornbread tests done with a toothpick and top is lightly browned.

Makes 9 servings.

Calories	205	Protein	3 g
Fat	7 g	Fiber	1 g
Cholesterol	26 mg	Sodium	470 mg
Carbohydrate	33 g		

Cornbread—Version 2

This cornbread is a bit darker in color than most cornbreads. That's because of the light brown sugar. This cornbread crumbles a bit, but not too much—just as you should expect.

Ingredients

1 egg
3/4 cup buttermilk
1/4 cup oil
1/3 cup potato starch
1/3 cup cornstarch
1 cup cornmeal
1/2 cup light brown sugar
1 1/2 teaspoons baking powder
1/2 teaspoon baking soda
3/4 teaspoon salt
3/4 teaspoon guar gum

Directions

Preheat oven to 375°. In medium bowl, combine egg, buttermilk, and oil. Mix well. Add all other ingredients and mix well, being sure to remove any lumps. Batter will be a bit thin.

Pour batter into greased 8 × 8 or 9 × 9 baking pan. Bake 25–29 minutes, until cornbread tests done with a toothpick and top is lightly browned.

Makes 9 large servings.

Calories	214	Protein	3 g
Fat	7 g	Fiber	1 g
Cholesterol	24 mg	Sodium	371 mg
Carbohydrate	35 g		

Cottage Dill Loaf

This loaf of bread is nice served with fish or chicken. It is mild yet quite flavorful.

Ingredients

1/2 cup milk, room temperature
1 packet yeast (about 1 tablespoon)
3/4 cup cottage cheese (small curd)
1/4 cup oil
3/4 cup potato starch
1 1/4 cups cornstarch
2 tablespoons sugar
1/2 teaspoon baking soda
2 teaspoons baking powder
2 1/2 teaspoons xanthan gum
1/2 teaspoon salt
1 tablespoon dried dill weed
1 1/4 teaspoons vinegar

Ingredient Alert—Most major brands of cottage cheese contain modified food starch and some even contain colorings. Consider purchasing certain store brands that do not contain modified food starch or colorings—a much better choice.

Directions

Preheat oven to 350°. In medium bowl, combine milk and yeast. Mix well to dissolve yeast. Add remaining ingredients, mixing well to remove all lumps. Dough will look wet, thick, and pasty.

Place dough into greased 9 × 4 loaf pan. Wet hands and smooth out top of dough, then press an indentation along center lengthwise of loaf. This step will make for a prettier loaf.

Bake 28–32 minutes. Loaf will be lightly browned. Test for doneness with a long toothpick, much as you would for a cake. Cool briefly before removing from pan. Refrigerate or freeze extra servings.

Makes 1 large loaf. Serves 10.

Calories	182	Protein	3 g
Fat	6 g	Fiber	2 g
Cholesterol	2 mg	Sodium	355 mg
Carbohydrate	29 g		

Chocolate Bread

This is a richly flavored loaf of bread. When first taken out of the oven, it seems too fragrant of cocoa but please don't be deterred; the aroma is deceptive. This recipe makes a very fine loaf of bread. The texture is wonderful, and the flavor is really good.

Ingredients

1 1/4 cups milk, room temperature
1 packet yeast (about 1 tablespoon)
1/4 cup molasses
1/4 cup oil
1 cup potato starch
1 1/4 cups cornstarch
1/4 cup cocoa
1 tablespoon baking powder
2 teaspoons xanthan gum

Directions

Preheat oven to 350°. In medium bowl, combine milk, yeast, and molasses. Stir to dissolve yeast. Add remaining ingredients. Mix well to remove all lumps. Dough will look wet, thick, and pasty.

Place dough into greased 9 × 4 loaf pan. Wet hands and smooth out top of dough. Make an indentation down middle of loaf. This will provide for a prettier loaf.

Bake 30 minutes. Test for doneness with a long toothpick, much as you would for a cake. Cool briefly before removing from pan. Refrigerate or freeze extra servings.

Makes 1 large loaf. Serves 10.

Calories	205	Protein	2 g
Fat	6 g	Fiber	2 g
Cholesterol	2 mg	Sodium	187 mg
Carbohydrate	35 g		

Egg Bread Loaf

This loaf of bread has the texture, the feel, and nearly the taste of regular bread. Even the crust is quite like regular bread. It is the lightest loaf of bread in this book. It takes well to the addition of herbs. In the other loaves of bread, I've shied away from using eggs, but not here. I wanted to use everything necessary to achieve the best possible combination! I hope you enjoy this loaf as much as our taste testers did. Oh, it's also a very pretty gluten-free loaf of bread.

Ingredients

- 1/4 cup shortening
- 3 tablespoons honey
- 2 eggs
- 1 packet yeast (about 1 tablespoon)
- 1 cup unflavored yogurt
- 1/2 cup potato starch
- 1 1/2 cups cornstarch
- 1/2 teaspoon baking soda
- 1 tablespoon baking powder
- 2 teaspoons xanthan gum
- 3/4 teaspoon salt
- 1 teaspoon vinegar

Directions

Preheat oven to 350°. Combine all ingredients. Mix well to remove all lumps.

The dough will be quite wet. Place dough in greased loaf pan. Smooth top with wet hands.

Bake 40–45 minutes, until loaf is lightly browned and toothpick inserted in middle tests clean.

Makes 1 large loaf. Serves 10.

Calories	197	Protein	3 g
Fat	7 g	Fiber	2 g
Cholesterol	44 mg	Sodium	414 mg
Carbohydrate	32 g		

English Muffins

Here is a recipe for the adventurous. The directions are lengthy, but each step is really quite easy.

Ingredients

2 tablespoons shortening
2 tablespoons sugar
1/2 cup water
1 packet yeast (about 1 tablespoon)
1/2 cup milk
3/4 cup potato starch
1 1/4 cups cornstarch
2 tablespoons oil
1/2 teaspoon baking soda
1 tablespoon baking powder
1 1/2 teaspoons xanthan gum
1/4 teaspoon vinegar

For tops and bottoms

2 tablespoons cornmeal (optional, but very helpful)

Directions

In medium bowl, combine shortening and sugar. Mix well. To sugar mixture, add water and yeast. Stir well to dissolve yeast. Add remaining ingredients. Mix well to remove all lumps.

Preheat griddle or large frying pan to low/medium heat. Grease muffin rings and pan. Place rings on pan. Sprinkle a bit of cornmeal where the base of the ring meets the pan. Pour about 1/3 cup batter into each ring. With moist or greased fingers, press batter evenly within the ring. Sprinkle a bit of cornmeal on top of each muffin. When lightly browned, only a few minutes, turn muffin over. Once browned on both sides,

Before you try this recipe, save a few short cans from your grocery shopping (pineapple slices, water chestnuts, etc.). You can use these cans, with tops and bottoms removed, as muffin rings. Or English muffin rings may be purchased from specialty shops, including several listed in the appendix.

lift ring to see that sides of muffin are cooked. If not, allow to cook a few minutes more. Remove muffin from pan and allow to cool completely.

If you like nooks and crannies, it is good to pull muffins apart with two forks back to back. Otherwise, just store in refrigerator or freezer until ready to use.

Makes 6–8 muffins. Serves 6.

Calories	274	Protein	1 g
Fat	9 g	Fiber	2 g
Cholesterol	2 mg	Sodium	387 mg
Carbohydrate	47 g		

Focaccia

Focaccia is a flat Italian bread. It looks like a dimpled pizza crust smothered with savory toppings. It is among the tastiest bread offerings in this book. Despite the fact that I love olive oil, it is used sparingly (only to sauté the onion) as it does not otherwise enhance this bread.

Ingredients

1/4 cup shortening
3 tablespoons honey
2 eggs
1 packet yeast (about 1 tablespoon)
1 cup unflavored yogurt, room temperature
1/2 cup potato starch
1 1/2 cups cornstarch
1/2 teaspoon baking soda
1 3/4 teaspoons baking powder
2 teaspoons xanthan gum
1 teaspoon salt
3/4 teaspoon vinegar

For topping

1 large onion, cut in half and thinly sliced
2 teaspoons olive oil
1 tablespoon fresh basil, finely chopped, or 1 teaspoon dried basil
1 tablespoon fresh oregano or 1 teaspoon dried oregano
1/2 teaspoon salt
1/8 teaspoon pepper (optional)

Directions

Preheat oven to 350°. Combine all ingredients. Mix well to remove all lumps.

This is a good opportunity to use Jane's Krazy Mixed-Up Salt to enhance the flavors of the toppings. It is a wonderful, one-shaker option to the spices and salt suggested in the toppings. It is my favorite spice combination and is gluten-free as of this writing.

The dough will be quite wet. Spread dough to 1/3–1/2 inch thickness on greased baking tin (approximately a 9 × 13 rectangle). Dough is easiest to spread with a spatula. Set aside.

In small skillet, fry onion in olive oil until soft.

Press indentations approximately 1-inch apart in dough. Place onions evenly over top of dough. Finally, sprinkle basil, oregano, salt, and pepper over top of onions.

Bake 15–20 minutes, until golden brown.

Serves 10.

Calories	215	Protein	3 g
Fat	8 g	Fiber	2 g
Cholesterol	44 mg	Sodium	508 mg
Carbohydrate	34 g		

Hot Cross Buns

I never made hot cross buns until my mother-in-law said that they were among her favorites. She's one of our favorite house-guests. We share a love of food, including a sweet tooth, and enjoy each other's company. I will make her hot cross buns any time she likes!

Ingredients

2 tablespoons shortening
1/3 cup sugar
1 packet yeast (about 1 tablespoon)
1 cup yogurt
1/4 cup oil
1/2 cup potato starch
1 cup cornstarch
1/4 teaspoon baking soda
2 teaspoons xanthan gum
1 tablespoon baking powder
1/2 teaspoon salt
1 1/2 teaspoons vanilla flavoring
1/4 teaspoon cinnamon
pinch of nutmeg
1/2 cup raisins (yellow raisins are nice)
2 teaspoons fresh orange zest, finely chopped

For icing

3/4 cup powdered sugar
1 1/2 tablespoons milk
few drops of vanilla flavoring

Directions

Preheat oven to 350°. In medium bowl, combine shortening and sugar. Mix well. Add yeast and yogurt. Mix well. Add all other ingredients, except raisins and orange zest. Mix well, being sure to remove all lumps. Fold in raisins and orange zest. Dough will be sticky and seemingly unmanageable.

Wet hands. Scoop about 1/4 cup of batter into hands. Shape into a ball and place onto lightly greased baking sheet or into greased muffin tins. Please note that the smoother the ball of dough, the smoother the crust on the baked bun.

Bake approximately 20 minutes, until tops are browned and a toothpick inserted in middle tests clean. Allow to cool for a few minutes.

Combine powdered sugar, milk, and vanilla flavoring. Drizzle over top of rolls in a cross pattern (traditional).

Makes 9 buns.

Calories	269	Protein	2 g
Fat	10 g	Fiber	3 g
Cholesterol	2 mg	Sodium	353 mg
Carbohydrate	45 g		

Pizza Crust

Here is a soft and chewy crust, or a thin and crispy crust. The choice is yours! It just depends on how thin you smooth out your dough. Please trust me on this and then enjoy.

Ingredients

1 packet yeast (about 1 tablespoon)
3/4 cup milk, room temperature
1/2 cup potato starch
3/4 cup cornstarch
1 tablespoon xanthan gum
1/4 teaspoon baking soda
1 teaspoon baking powder
1/2 teaspoon salt
1/4 cup shortening

Directions

Preheat oven to 375°. In small bowl, combine yeast and milk. Stir to dissolve yeast. Set aside.

In medium bowl, combine all dry ingredients and shortening. Mix well.

To dry ingredients, slowly add milk/yeast mixture. Mix well. Dough will look wet, thick, and pasty but is quite workable if you spray your hands with nonstick spray or keep your hands damp with water. This is a soft dough.

Roll or pat out dough onto a lightly greased baking tin or pizza pan. For a thick crust, pat out dough to 1/4 inch thickness. For a thin crust, pat out dough to 1/8 inch thickness. A 12-inch circle will produce a "hand-tossed" thickness—not too thick, not too thin.

Consider baking this crust and freezing it without toppings. Then you only have to thaw, top, and bake briefly.

Top as desired.

Bake 15–25 minutes, until crust is lightly browned. Use a spatula to lift up the pizza to check for light browning on the bottom of the crust the first time you make it.

Calories	202	Protein	2 g
Fat	9 g	Fiber	4 g
Cholesterol	2 mg	Sodium	337 mg
Carbohydrate	28 g		

Rolls

These rolls are fashioned after traditional white dinner rolls. Because they are baked in a muffin tin, they look a lot like popovers. They are mild, very light, and will probably surprise you because they are so good. Let them cool a minute or two after taking them from the oven.

Ingredients

4	tablespoons shortening
3	tablespoons honey
2	eggs
1	packet yeast (about 1 tablespoon)
1	cup sour cream
1/2	cup potato starch
1	cup cornstarch
1/2	teaspoon baking soda
1	tablespoon baking powder
2	teaspoons xanthan gum
3/4	teaspoon salt
3/4	teaspoon vinegar

Directions

Preheat oven to 350°. Combine all ingredients. Mix well to remove all lumps.

The dough will be quite wet. Wet hands to handle dough. Take about 1/4 cup of dough and shape into a ball. Drop into greased baking tin. Repeat until all dough is used.

Bake 18–20 minutes, until golden brown and toothpick inserted in middle tests clean.

Makes 9 rolls.

Calories	222	Protein	2 g
Fat	11 g	Fiber	2 g
Cholesterol	56 mg	Sodium	452 mg
Carbohydrate	28 g		

Sourdough Loaf

This loaf has just a bit of a kick. If you like sourdough, you'll enjoy this bread.

Ingredients

1 1/4 cup cornstarch, divided
1/2 cup water, room temperature
1 packet yeast (about 1 tablespoon)
2 tablespoons sugar
1 teaspoon salt
1 1/4 cups potato starch
1/4 cup oil
1 tablespoon baking powder
2 teaspoons xanthan gum
3/4 cup milk, room temperature

Directions

Preheat oven to 350°. In medium bowl, combine 1/2 cup cornstarch, water, yeast, sugar, and salt. Mix well. Allow to sit at room temperature overnight. The time is needed to develop the sourdough flavor. To yeast mixture, add remaining ingredients. Mix well. Dough will look wet, thick, and pasty.

Place dough into greased 9 × 4 loaf pan. Wet hands and smooth out top of dough, then make an indentation down the center lengthwise of loaf. This will provide for a prettier loaf.

Bake 25–28 minutes. Loaf will just begin to brown. Test for doneness with a long toothpick, much as you would for a cake. Cool briefly before removing from pan. Refrigerate or freeze extra servings.

Makes 1 large loaf. Serves 10.

Calories	196	Protein	1 g
Fat	6 g	Fiber	2 g
Cholesterol	1 mg	Sodium	386 mg
Carbohydrate	35 g		

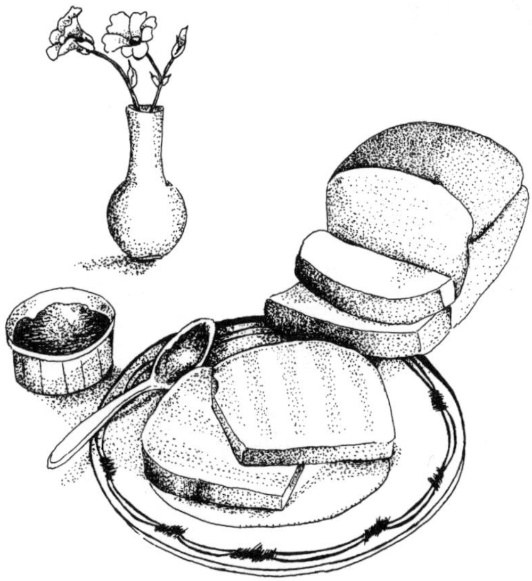

CHAPTER 5

Quick Breads

Baking gluten-free quick breads is a snap. Batters will look different, ingredients may seem odd, and finished breads will be delicious.

Mixing gluten-free quick breads requires special attention in two areas. First, please use a mixer. A hand-held mixer is perfectly fine. Using a mixer will enable you to remove virtually all the lumps from the batter. This is important as flour clumps may remain after baking. You cannot overmix these quick breads, unlike their wheat-containing counterparts. So don't let that be a concern. Second, batters will often stick to the sides of a mixing bowl. It is best to scrape down the sides of the mixing bowl with a spatula once or twice during mixing.

Once baked, your gluten-free breads and muffins need appropriate storage. Please wrap them well and refrigerate them after they cool. A few of the breads retain their original moisture/texture best when frozen on the day of baking and are so noted.

So, now you're ready to bake but don't know which recipe to try first? They are all good, but I'm especially partial to the Cranberry-Orange Bread and the Pumpkin Bread.

Apple Muffins

Looking for something just a tad sweet? Well, here it is. These muffins have a wonderful high dome. They can be made in just a few minutes.

Ingredients

1/2 cup sugar
1/4 cup shortening
1 egg
3/4 cup cornstarch
1/2 cup potato starch
3/4 cup milk
2 teaspoons baking powder
1/4 teaspoon baking soda
1/2 teaspoon salt
1/2 teaspoon cinnamon
scant 1/2 teaspoon xanthan gum
1 small apple, peeled, cored, and grated (about 1/2 cup packed)

For topping

1 tablespoon sugar

My secret for grating an apple is to peel it but not core it. I then grate it until I have nothing left but core.

Directions

Preheat oven to 350°. In medium bowl, combine sugar and shortening. Mix well. Add egg. Mix well. Add all other ingredients except for apple and mix well. Be sure to remove all lumps from batter. Fold in apple.

Fill greased muffin tins (or tins with paper liners) about 2/3 full. Sprinkle small amount of sugar over top of each muffin.

Bake 18–20 minutes, until toothpick inserted in muffin tests clean. Top of muffin should not look wet.

Makes 8–9 muffins. Serves 8.

Calories	214	Protein	2 g
Fat	8 g	Fiber	1 g
Cholesterol	28 mg	Sodium	327 mg
Carbohydrate	36 g		

Banana Bread

I looked literally for years to find a banana bread recipe that was moist but not doughy. Here is my gluten-free version of that recipe. This loaf is soft and light. If you prefer a heavier banana bread, please try the Banana Muffins.

Ingredients

2	small bananas (up to 3/4 cup)
1	egg
1/2	cup light brown sugar
1/4	cup oil
1/2	cup milk
1/2	teaspoon vanilla flavoring
1/2	cup potato starch
1/2	cup cornstarch
4	teaspoons baking powder
1	teaspoon guar gum
1/4	teaspoon baking soda
1	teaspoon ground coriander (optional, but adds great flavor)
1/4	teaspoon salt

Directions

Preheat oven to 350°. In large bowl, mash bananas well. Add egg, light brown sugar, oil, milk, and vanilla flavoring. Mix well. Add potato starch, cornstarch, baking powder, guar gum, baking soda, salt, and coriander. Mix well. Batter will be thin.

Pour into greased 9 × 4 loaf pan. Bake approximately 40 minutes, until toothpick inserted in middle tests clean. Allow to cool briefly before removing from pan. Refrigerate or freeze extra servings. Keep covered to prevent drying out.

Makes 1 large loaf. Serves 10.

Calories	178	Protein	1 g
Fat	6 g	Fiber	1 g
Cholesterol	22 mg	Sodium	316 mg
Carbohydrate	29 g		

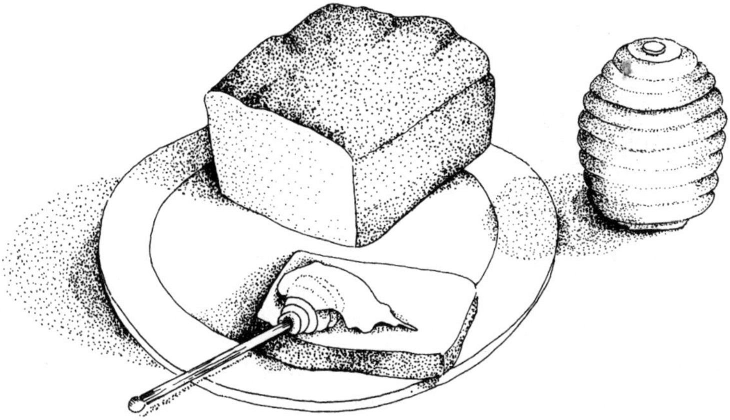

Banana Muffins

Here is a moist, heavier muffin with lots of banana flavor.

Ingredients

1 large mashed banana (about 1/2 cup)
1/4 cup shortening
1/2 cup sugar
1 egg
2/3 cup potato starch
1 cup cornstarch
2 1/4 teaspoons baking powder
3/4 teaspoon baking soda
2/3 cup milk
1/2 teaspoon salt
1 teaspoon vanilla flavoring
1/2 teaspoon xanthan gum

For topping

1 tablespoon brown sugar

Directions

Preheat oven to 350°. In medium bowl, mash banana well. To banana, add shortening, sugar, and egg. Mix well. Add remaining ingredients and mix well, being sure to remove all lumps from the batter.

Fill greased muffin tins (or tins with paper liners) about 2/3 full. Sprinkle a small amount of brown sugar on top of each muffin.

Bake 15–20 minutes, until lightly browned and a toothpick tests clean when inserted in muffin. Freeze extra muffins.

Makes 10–12 muffins. Serves 10.

Calories	197	Protein	1 g
Fat	6 g	Fiber	1 g
Cholesterol	23 mg	Sodium	338 mg
Carbohydrate	35 g		

Blueberry Muffins

These muffins are fluffy and a bit homely looking, but they sure do taste good. Bet you can't eat just one!

Ingredients

1/4 cup sugar
2 tablespoons shortening
1 egg
1/4 cup oil
1/2 cup potato starch
3/4 cup cornstarch
1/4 teaspoon baking soda
1 1/2 teaspoons xanthan gum
1 tablespoon baking powder
2/3 cup milk
1/2 teaspoon salt
1 teaspoon vanilla flavoring
1 1/2 cups blueberries

For topping

1 tablespoon sugar
1/4 teaspoon cinnamon (optional)

Directions

Preheat oven to 350°. In medium bowl, cream together sugar and shortening. Add remaining ingredients except blueberries and mix well. Be sure no lumps remain. Gently fold in blueberries.

Pour batter into greased muffin tins or pans with paper liners. Fill cups about 2/3 full. Sprinkle with sugar/cinnamon mixture.

Bake 20–23 minutes, until toothpick tests clean and tops are lightly browned.

Makes 12 muffins.

Calories	156	Protein	1 g
Fat	8 g	Fiber	2 g
Cholesterol	19 mg	Sodium	262 mg
Carbohydrate	21 g		

Cranberry-Orange Bread

This bread is medium-bodied and full of flavor. It is a very pretty bread with just a hint of sweetness. It cuts better when allowed to cool, but I find it hard to wait.

Ingredients

1 egg
1/2 cup sugar
1/4 cup oil
1/2 cup orange juice
1/2 cup milk
2/3 cup potato starch
1 cup cornstarch
1 tablespoon baking powder
3/4 teaspoon xanthan gum
1/4 teaspoon baking soda
1/2 teaspoon salt
2/3 cup finely chopped cranberries

For topping

1 teaspoon sugar

Cranberries are easiest to chop in a food processor if they are frozen first and sprinkled with a small amount of the sugar used in the recipe.

Directions

Preheat oven to 350°. In medium bowl, combine egg, sugar, oil, orange juice, and milk. Mix well. Add all remaining ingredients except for cranberries and mix well to remove all lumps from batter. Fold in cranberries.

Pour batter into large greased loaf pan. Sprinkle 1 teaspoon sugar over top of batter.

Bake approximately 40 minutes, until toothpick inserted in bread tests clean. Top will be lightly browned. Allow to cool in pan for at least 5 minutes before removing from pan. Freeze extra portions.

Makes 1 large loaf. Serves 10.

Calories	193	Protein	1 g
Fat	6 g	Fiber	1 g
Cholesterol	22 mg	Sodium	312 mg
Carbohydrate	33 g		

Nut Bread

This is a medium-bodied loaf. It has my favorite nut combination of pecans and vanilla. Feel free to substitute a heartier nut, such as black walnuts, if you prefer.

Ingredients

1 egg
3/4 cup light brown sugar
1/4 cup oil
1 cup milk
1 teaspoon vanilla flavoring
2/3 cup potato starch
1 cup cornstarch
1 tablespoon baking powder
3/4 teaspoon xanthan gum
3/4 teaspoon baking soda
1/2 teaspoon salt
2/3 cup ground pecans

For topping

1 teaspoon sugar

Directions

Preheat oven to 350°. In medium bowl, combine egg, light brown sugar, oil, milk, and vanilla flavoring. Mix well. Add all other ingredients except for nuts and mix well to remove all lumps from batter. Fold in nuts.

Pour batter into 9 × 4 greased loaf pan. Sprinkle 1 teaspoon sugar over top of batter. Bake approximately 40–45 minutes, until toothpick inserted in bread tests clean. Top will be browned. Allow to cool in pan for at least 5 minutes before removing from pan. Freeze extra servings.

Makes 1 large loaf. Serves 10.

Calories	273	Protein	2 g
Fat	12 g	Fiber	1 g
Cholesterol	23 mg	Sodium	388 mg
Carbohydrate	41 g		

Pumpkin Bread

Forget saving pumpkin for the holidays; this bread is nice anytime you want something special but not too rich. This bread has a sweet, almost crisp crust with a moist, medium-textured center. I was going to send this to the taste testers, but it never made it out the door!

Ingredients

3/4 cup canned pumpkin
1 egg
3/4 cup light brown sugar
1/4 cup oil
1/4 cup evaporated milk
1/2 cup potato starch
3/4 cup cornstarch
1/4 teaspoon baking soda
1 tablespoon baking powder
1/2 teaspoon salt
1 teaspoon guar gum
1/2 teaspoon cinnamon
1/4 teaspoon nutmeg
pinch (1/8 teaspoon) cloves (optional)

Directions

Preheat oven to 350°. In large bowl, combine pumpkin, egg, light brown sugar, oil, and milk. Mix well. Add remaining ingredients. Mix well to remove any lumps in batter.

Pour batter into 9 × 4 greased loaf pan. Bake 40–45 minutes, until toothpick inserted in bread tests clean. Allow bread to cool in pan for at least 5 minutes. Freeze extra portions.

Makes 1 large loaf. Serves 10.

Calories	203	Protein	1 g
Fat	7 g	Fiber	1 g
Cholesterol	23 mg	Sodium	320 mg
Carbohydrate	35 g		

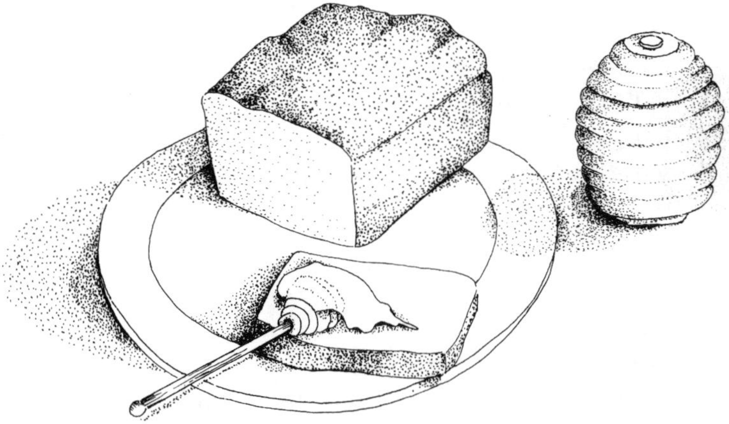

Pumpkin Spice Muffins

I think pumpkin is an underused vegetable. It adds flavor and moisture to cakes and muffins. Although this recipe uses just a portion of a can of pumpkin, these muffins are really nice.

Ingredients

1/4 cup shortening
1/2 cup sugar
3/4 cup cornstarch
1/2 cup potato starch
1/2 cup milk
1/2 cup pumpkin
1 egg
2 teaspoons baking powder
1/4 teaspoon baking soda
1/2 teaspoon salt
1/2 teaspoon cinnamon
1/4 teaspoon nutmeg
1/4 teaspoon ginger
scant 1/2 teaspoon xanthan gum

For topping

1 tablespoon sugar

Directions

Preheat oven to 350°. In medium bowl, combine shortening and sugar. Mix well. Add all other ingredients and mix well. Be sure to remove all lumps from batter. Fill greased muffin tins (or tins with paper liners) about 2/3 full. Sprinkle small amount of sugar over top of each muffin.

Bake 18–20 minutes, until toothpick inserted in muffin tests clean. Top of muffin should not look wet.

Makes 8–9 muffins. Serves 8.

Calories	209	Protein	2 g
Fat	7 g	Fiber	1 g
Cholesterol	28 mg	Sodium	324 mg
Carbohydrate	35 g		

Applesauce Quick Bread

Here is a delightful snack. It is a soft and understated quick bread—real pleasant.

Ingredients

1 cup applesauce
1 egg
1/2 cup sugar
1/4 cup oil
1/4 cup milk
3/4 cup potato starch
3/4 cup cornstarch
1/4 teaspoon baking soda
1/2 teaspoon salt
1 tablespoon baking powder
1/2 teaspoon cinnamon
1 1/4 teaspoons guar gum

Directions

Preheat oven to 350°. In large bowl, combine applesauce, egg, sugar, oil, and milk. Mix well. Add all remaining ingredients, mixing well to remove all lumps. Batter will be thin. Pour into greased 9 × 4 loaf pan.

Bake 40–45 minutes, until toothpick inserted in bread tests clean.

Makes 1 large loaf. Serves 10.

Calories	185	Protein	1 g
Fat	6 g	Fiber	0 g
Cholesterol	22 mg	Sodium	309 mg
Carbohydrate	32 g		

Savory Hush Puppies

These are the heavier, more robust hush puppies often served alongside casual fish or seafood meals.

Ingredients

1/2	cup potato starch
1/2	cup cornstarch
1/2	cup cornmeal
1	tablespoon sugar
1	teaspoon baking powder
1/4	teaspoon baking soda
1	egg
1/2	cup buttermilk
1/2	teaspoon xanthan gum
	pinch salt (1/8 teaspoon)
1 1/4	cups finely chopped onion

Directions

In medium bowl, combine all ingredients. Mix until well blended and no lumps remain.

Drop by rounded teaspoonful into hot oil (375°). Turn as needed until medium golden brown. Drain on paper towels.

Makes about 20 hush puppies. Serves 5.

Calories	288	Protein	4 g
Fat	11 g	Fiber	3 g
Cholesterol	44 mg	Sodium	237 mg
Carbohydrate	43 g		

Strawberry Shortcake

The recommended base for this old-fashioned shortcake is Sweet Biscuit Dough. That is the kind my mother served when I was little. If you prefer a sponge-type base, use a slice or two of Sponge Cake in its place.

Recommended base

Sweet Biscuits (page 129) *or*
Sponge Cake (prepared and freshly baked), (page 164)

For toppings

1 pint fresh berries, washed, hulled, and sliced
Whipped Cream (page 264)

Directions

Prepare Sweet Biscuit dough and bake. Set aside. Prepare strawberries. Set aside.

When ready to serve, split biscuits. Fill with strawberries. Cover with top half of biscuit. Place more strawberries on top. Finally, top with whipped cream. Serve right away.

Serves 9.

Calories	276	Protein	1 g
Fat	18 g	Fiber	2 g
Cholesterol	39 mg	Sodium	352 mg
Carbohydrate	28 g		

Sweet Biscuits

This sweet biscuit dough is used in Strawberry Shortcake and various cobblers.

Ingredients

- 1/3 cup shortening
- 1/4 cup sugar
- 1/2 cup potato starch
- 3/4 cup cornstarch
- 1/4 teaspoon baking soda
- 1 1/2 teaspoon xanthan gum
- 1 tablespoon baking powder
- 2/3 cup milk
- 1/2 teaspoon salt
- 1/2 teaspoon vanilla flavoring

Directions

Preheat oven to 375°. In medium bowl, cream together shortening and sugar. Add remaining ingredients and mix until all lumps are removed. Batter will be quite soft and sticky.

If not using in another recipe and baking them plain, pat out dough to 1/2-inch thickness on "floured"—with cornstarch—surface. Cut out 2 1/2 inch round circles and place on greased baking sheet.

Bake 12–15 minutes, until tops are very lightly browned.

Makes about 9 biscuits.

Calories	169	Protein	1 g
Fat	8 g	Fiber	1 g
Cholesterol	1 mg	Sodium	341 mg
Carbohydrate	24 g		

Zucchini Bread

Here is a tasty zucchini bread this is made without the large quantity of oil called for in most other zucchini bread recipes.

Ingredients

1	egg
3	tablespoons oil
2	tablespoons shortening
3/4	cup sugar
1	teaspoon vanilla flavoring
1/2	cup potato starch
3/4	cup cornstarch
1	tablespoon baking powder
3/4	teaspoon baking soda
1/4	teaspoon salt
3/4	teaspoon xanthan gum
1	teaspoon cinnamon
1/4	cup milk
1	cup grated zucchini, packed

Directions

Preheat oven to 350°. In large bowl, combine egg, oil, shortening, sugar, and vanilla flavoring. Mix well. Add all remaining ingredients except zucchini. Mix well to remove all lumps. Batter will be thick. Add zucchini and mix well.

Pour batter into greased 9 × 4 loaf pan. Bake 45 minutes, until toothpick inserted in bread tests clean. Allow to cool in pan for at least 10 minutes. Freeze extra portions.

Makes 1 large loaf. Serves 10.

Calories	192	Protein	1 g
Fat	7 g	Fiber	1 g
Cholesterol	22 mg	Sodium	318 mg
Carbohydrate	31 g		

Sweet Hush Puppies

There's a family-style restaurant near my home that serves just-sweet-enough hush puppies alongside their fried chicken. This recipe was inspired by their fine hush puppies.

Ingredients

1/2 cup potato starch
3/4 cup cornstarch
2 tablespoons sugar
1 teaspoon baking powder
1/4 teaspoon baking soda
1 egg
1/3 cup buttermilk
1/2 teaspoon xanthan gum
1/4 teaspoon cinnamon
1/4 teaspoon vanilla
pinch salt (1/8 teaspoon)

For topping

1/2 cup powdered sugar

Directions

In medium bowl, combine all ingredients. Mix until well blended and no lumps remain.

Drop by rounded teaspoonful into hot oil (375°). Turn as needed until medium golden brown. Drain on paper towels.

While still warm, roll in or sprinkle on powdered sugar.

Makes about 20 hush puppies. Serves 5.

Calories	290	Protein	2 g
Fat	11 g	Fiber	1 g
Cholesterol	43 mg	Sodium	256 mg
Carbohydrate	46 g		

CHAPTER 6

Cakes

I am so pleased to share this chapter with you! For every child who wants his or her birthday cake to be just like everyone else's, for anyone who wants a special dessert to share with the rest of the crowd, and for those of you who just want to eat cake, this chapter is for you.

When I first began writing this chapter, my favorite cake was absolutely the Carrot Cake, with the Sponge Cake being a close second. But then the Gingerbread got rave reviews. And the Red Velvet Cake tastes just like my grandma's. And, of course, the Chocolate Cake is hard to beat. So I guess I really can't tell you which cake is the best. You'll have to decide for yourself.

In making these cakes, batters may seem unusually thin or even unusually thick. These batter oddities are necessary to duplicate exactly the flavors and textures of the finished cakes. You will be pleased.

As often mentioned in this book, please be sure to mix your cake batters well to remove all lumps. These lumps rarely dissolve in baking, even if the batter is quite thin.

Baking time needs to be closely watched the first few times cake recipes are used because underbaking will give you undesirable wet spots, and overbaking will give you a dry cake. And the right baking time will give you a terrific cake.

Several recipes in this chapter suggest that extra portions be frozen to retain their fresh-baked texture and moisture. This is important as these particular cakes dry out quickly if only refrigerated or kept at room temperature for more than a day.

Buttercream Icing

This is the traditional homemade icing made by many home bakers. You may notice that I use a bit more butter, but that additional butter really makes the icing special.

For full-sized cake

3/4 cup butter, softened
3 3/4 cups powdered sugar (1 pound)
2 teaspoons vanilla flavoring
up to 1/4 cup milk or cream

For petite cake

6 tablespoons butter, softened
2 cups powdered sugar
1 teaspoon vanilla flavoring
up to 2 tablespoons milk or cream

Directions

In medium bowl, cream butter and sugar until well blended. Add vanilla flavoring. Slowly add enough milk to bring icing to spreading consistency. Continue beating icing for at least 3–5 minutes. Apply to fully cooled cake.

Calories	528	Protein	1 g
Fat	25 g	Fiber	0 g
Cholesterol	67 mg	Sodium	11 mg
Carbohydrate	80 g		

Angel Food Cake

This angel food cake is preferred in our house over traditional angel food cake. It is light yet not too sweet.

Ingredients

1/2 cup cornstarch
1/3 cup potato starch
3/4 teaspoon guar gum
3/4 cup sugar
1/2 teaspoon salt
1 1/4 cup egg whites
1 tablespoon water
1 teaspoon cream of tartar
2 teaspoons vanilla flavoring
1/3 cup sugar

Directions

Preheat oven to 350°. In medium bowl, combine cornstarch, potato starch, guar gum, 3/4 cup sugar, and salt. Set aside. In large mixing bowl, combine egg whites, water, cream of tartar, and vanilla. Mix until frothy. While continuing to beat egg white mixture, slowly beat in 1/3 cup sugar. Continue beating until stiff peaks are formed. Fold in flour mixture, making sure no lumps remain.

Pour batter into ungreased angel food cake pan. Press batter down slightly to remove any large air spaces. Bake 35–40 minutes, until light golden brown.

Invert pan over glass bottle. This cake cools upside down. Once cool, remove from pan.

Makes 1 large cake. Serves 12.

Calories	117	Protein	3 g
Fat	0 g	Fiber	0 g
Cholesterol	0 mg	Sodium	135 mg
Carbohydrate	26 g		

Boston Cream Pie

I've never known why this is called "pie," but it is delicious.

Ingredients

2/3 cup cornstarch
2/3 cup potato starch
2 teaspoons baking powder
1/2 teaspoon salt
1 teaspoon guar gum
2/3 cup sugar
1 egg
3 tablespoons oil
1 teaspoon vanilla flavoring
1/2 teaspoon baking soda
3/4 cup milk

For filling

1/4 cup sugar
1 1/2 tablespoons cornstarch
1/4 teaspoon salt
1 cup milk
1 egg
1 teaspoon vanilla flavoring

For chocolate glaze

1/4 cup cocoa
1/4 cup butter
1 cup powdered sugar
1 teaspoon vanilla flavoring

Directions

Preheat oven to 350°. In medium bowl, combine all ingredients, except milk. While stirring, slowly add milk. Be sure all lumps are removed. Pour batter into greased 8-inch round pan. Bake 25–30 minutes, until toothpick tests clean. Cool.

In small saucepan, combine all ingredients for filling. Constantly stir while cooking over low heat until filling thickens. Pour filling into small bowl and cover with plastic wrap touching the filling; this prevents a "skin" from forming. Cool.

In small saucepan, combine all ingredients for glaze. Constantly stir while cooking over low heat. Allow to boil for a minute or two. Cool to room temperature.

Split cake in half to form two thin layers. Assemble final cake by placing filling atop bottom layer of cake. Cover with second layer of cake. Pour glaze over top.

Makes 8 servings.

Calories	385	Protein	4 g
Fat	14 g	Fiber	0 g
Cholesterol	74 mg	Sodium	458 mg
Carbohydrate	61 g		

Carrot Cake

We were encouraging my sister's family to taste-test this cake when they were visiting. (Anyone who walks through my front door is forced to try my latest creations.) My teenage nephew said he wouldn't try it unless his sister tried it first. Being a wonderful girl, she did. With a look of astonishment, she said, "Mmm, this is really good. It tastes just like regular carrot cake." My sister, her husband, and their now brave son echoed the same appreciation of the cake. It is very moist but not wet, just like it should be.

Ingredients

1/2	cup oil
1/2	cup sugar
1/2	cup dark brown sugar
2	eggs
3/4	cup cornstarch
2/3	cup potato starch
3/4	teaspoon baking soda
1/2	teaspoon baking powder
1	teaspoon cinnamon
1/2	teaspoon salt
1/2	teaspoon xanthan gum
3	tablespoons water
1/2	cup chopped nuts (optional)
1 1/2	cups packed grated carrots (about 4 medium carrots)

For icing

2	cups powdered sugar
3	ounces cream cheese
2	tablespoons butter, softened
1	teaspoon vanilla flavoring
	a few drops of milk

Directions

Preheat oven to 300°. In a large bowl, combine oil, sugar, and dark brown sugar. Mix well. Add all remaining ingredients except for the nuts and carrots. Mix well, being sure that no lumps remain in the batter. Mix in carrots and nuts.

Pour batter into greased 8 × 8 or 9 × 9 baking pan. Bake 45–55 minutes, until toothpick inserted in center tests clean. Note that this cake will have a bit of a dome when first removed from the oven. It will settle as it cools.

For icing, combine powdered sugar, cream cheese, butter, and vanilla. Beat very well. Add a few drops of milk as needed. Spread icing on cooled cake. Freeze extra portions.

Makes one cake. Serves 9.

Calories	446	Protein	2 g
Fat	20 g	Fiber	1 g
Cholesterol	65 mg	Sodium	310 mg
Carbohydrate	67 g		

Chocolate Buttercream Icing

This is the chocolate version of traditional homemade icing.

For full-sized cake

2 ounces unsweetened chocolate, chopped in small pieces
3/4 cup butter, softened
3 3/4 cups powdered sugar (1 pound)
2 teaspoons vanilla flavoring
up to 1/4 cup milk or cream

For petite cake

1 ounce unsweetened chocolate, chopped in small pieces
6 tablespoons butter, softened
2 cups powdered sugar
1 teaspoon vanilla flavoring
up to 2 tablespoons milk or cream

Directions

In small, microwavable bowl or cup or a double boiler, melt chocolate. Set aside to cool.

In medium bowl, cream butter and sugar until well blended. Add vanilla flavoring. Slowly add enough milk to bring icing to spreading consistency. Slowly beat in cooled chocolate. Continue beating icing for at least 3–5 minutes.

Apply to fully cooled cake.

Calories	576	Protein	2 g
Fat	30 g	Fiber	0 g
Cholesterol	67 mg	Sodium	11 mg
Carbohydrate	82 g		

Chocolate Pound Cake

This cake is chocolaty good. A sprinkle of powdered sugar is all the accompaniment needed. However, Whipped Cream and a cup of hot chocolate would be a great chocolate fix.

Ingredients

1/2 cup softened butter
1 cup sugar
2 eggs
1 1/2 teaspoons vanilla flavoring
1/2 cup cornstarch
1/2 cup potato starch
1/2 cup cocoa
2 1/2 teaspoons baking powder
3/4 teaspoon salt
1 1/8 teaspoons guar gum
3/4 cup milk

Directions

Preheat oven to 350°. In large bowl, cream together butter and sugar. Add eggs and vanilla flavoring. Mix well. Add all remaining ingredients except milk. Mix well, being sure to remove all lumps. Slowly mix in milk.

Pour batter into greased 9 × 4 loaf pan. Bake 50 minutes, until toothpick inserted in middle of loaf tests clean. Allow cake to cool in pan for at least 10 minutes.

Makes 1 large loaf. Serves 10.

Calories	254	Protein	3 g
Fat	12 g	Fiber	0 g
Cholesterol	70 mg	Sodium	318 mg
Carbohydrate	35 g		

Chocolate Cake

This is a traditional moist, fluffy cake, much like that from a traditional cake mix.

Ingredients

1/2 cup cocoa
1/2 cup boiling water
1 cup cornstarch
1 1/4 cups potato starch
1 tablespoon plus 1 1/2 teaspoons baking powder
1 teaspoon salt
2 1/2 teaspoons guar gum
1 cup sugar
2 eggs
1/4 cup oil
2 teaspoons vanilla flavoring
1 1/4 cups milk, divided

Did you know? Boiling water is used to release the flavor of the cocoa.

Directions

Preheat oven to 350°. In large bowl, combine cocoa and boiling water. Mix well. Add all other ingredients, except for 1 cup milk. Mix well to remove all lumps from batter. Slowly add remaining 1 cup milk. Mix well. Batter will be quite thin at first but will thicken a bit with continued mixing.

Pour batter into two greased 8- or 9-inch round pans or one greased 9 × 13 rectangular pan. Bake 22–25 minutes, until toothpick inserted in middle of cake tests clean.

Makes 1 layer or rectangular cake. Serves 15.

Calories	193	Protein	2 g
Fat	5 g	Fiber	0 g
Cholesterol	30 mg	Sodium	323 mg
Carbohydrate	35 g		

Chocolate Angel Food Cake

This angel food cake is moist, light, and chocolaty. It was inspired by Rose Bernbaum's Chocolate Angel Food Cake in The Cake Bible. *This cake does not have the height of the plain Angel Food Cake, but its understated richness more than makes up for any loss of stature.*

Ingredients

1/4 cup cornstarch
1/4 cup potato starch
1/4 cup cocoa
1/2 teaspoon guar gum
3/4 cup sugar
1/2 teaspoon salt
1 1/4 cups egg whites
1 tablespoon water
1 teaspoon cream of tartar
1 teaspoon vanilla flavoring
1/3 cup sugar

Directions

Preheat oven to 350°. In medium bowl, combine cornstarch, potato starch, cocoa, guar gum, 3/4 cup sugar, and salt. Set aside.

In large mixing bowl, combine egg whites, water, cream of tartar, and vanilla flavoring. Mix until frothy. While continuing to beat egg white mixture, slowly beat in 1/3 cup sugar. Continue beating until stiff peaks are formed. Fold in flour mixture, making sure no lumps remain.

Pour batter into ungreased angel food cake pan. Press batter down slightly to remove any large air spaces. Bake 35–40 minutes, until light golden brown.

Invert pan over glass bottle. This cake cools upside down. Once cool, remove from pan.

Makes 1 cake. Serves 12.

Calories	110	Protein	3 g
Fat	0 g	Fiber	0 g
Cholesterol	0 mg	Sodium	135 mg
Carbohydrate	24 g		

Chocolate Velvet Icing

This recipe is among my favorites. It is a very understated chocolate icing that can complete a "chocolate fix" when put atop a chocolate cake. Yet it is not too strong to complement a yellow cake.

For full-sized cake

1 cup milk
2 ounces unsweetened chocolate, chopped in small pieces
2 1/2 tablespoons cornstarch
1 cup butter
1 cup sugar
2 teaspoons vanilla flavoring

For petite cake

1/2 cup milk
1 ounce unsweetened chocolate, chopped in small pieces
1 tablespoon plus 3/4 teaspoon cornstarch
1/2 cup butter
1/2 cup sugar
1 teaspoon vanilla flavoring

Directions

In microwave-safe bowl, combine milk, chocolate, and cornstarch. Stir well. Microwave this mixture on high for 2–4 minutes, until quite thick. Stop and stir well every minute or so. The milk, chocolate, and cornstarch may also be cooked in a saucepan over medium heat. Stir constantly if using this method.

Cover milk mixture with plastic wrap touching its surface. This will prevent "skin" from forming. Cool to room temperature.

In medium bowl, cream butter, sugar, and vanilla flavoring until light and fluffy.

Add milk mixture and beat until frosting looks like whipped cream. This will take several minutes.

Calories	492	Protein	3 g
Fat	38 g	Fiber	1 g
Cholesterol	91 mg	Sodium	26 mg
Carbohydrate	40 g		

Gingerbread

Warning: this gingerbread got rave reviews from my taste testers.

Ingredients

1/3 cup molasses
1/3 cup light corn syrup
2/3 cup boiling water
3/4 cup cornstarch
1/2 cup plus 2 tablespoons potato starch
1 1/4 teaspoons baking soda
3/4 teaspoon baking powder
1 teaspoon cinnamon
1 teaspoon ginger
1/2 teaspoon salt
3/4 teaspoon xanthan gum
1/3 cup oil
1/3 cup sugar
1 egg

Directions

Preheat oven to 325°. In small bowl, combine molasses, light corn syrup, and boiling water. Set aside to cool.

In large bowl, combine cornstarch, potato starch, baking soda, baking powder, cinnamon, ginger, salt, and xanthan gum. To flour mixture, add oil, sugar, egg, and cooled molasses mixture. Mix well to remove all lumps.

Pour batter into greased 8 × 8 or 9 × 9 pan. Bake 40 minutes, until toothpick inserted in middle of cake tests done.

Makes 9 large servings.

Calories	244	Protein	1 g
Fat	9 g	Fiber	1 g
Cholesterol	24 mg	Sodium	374 mg
Carbohydrate	42 g		

Pecan Cake

You may be surprised at the delicate flavor of this cake. If you prefer a heartier nut taste, substitute ground walnuts for the ground pecans and omit the vanilla flavoring.

Ingredients

1 1/3 cups cornstarch
1 cup potato starch
1/2 cup ground pecans
1 1/2 tablespoons baking powder
1 teaspoon salt
2 teaspoons xanthan gum
1 cup sugar
2 eggs
1/4 cup oil
2 teaspoons vanilla flavoring
1 3/4 cups milk

Directions

Preheat oven to 350°. In large bowl, combine all ingredients except milk. Mix well to remove all lumps. Slowly mix in milk.

Pour batter into 2 greased 8- or 9-inch round pans or 1 greased 9 × 13 rectangular pan. Bake 23–28 minutes, until toothpick inserted in middle of cake tests clean. Do not use browning to indicate doneness. Freeze extra portions.

Makes 1 large cake. Serves 15.

Calories	220	Protein	2 g
Fat	8 g	Fiber	2 g
Cholesterol	31 mg	Sodium	326 mg
Carbohydrate	35 g		

Petite Chocolate Cake

This is my favorite chocolate cake in this book. It is really moist and chocolatey with a nice, tight texture.

Ingredients

1/2	cup cornstarch
1/3	cup potato starch
1/2	cup cocoa
1	teaspoon baking powder
1/2	teaspoon salt
1	teaspoon guar gum
2/3	cup sugar
1	egg
3	tablespoons oil
1	teaspoon vanilla flavoring
1/2	teaspoon baking soda
3/4	cup milk

Directions

Preheat oven to 350°. In medium bowl, combine all ingredients except milk. While stirring, slowly add milk. Be sure all lumps are removed.

Pour batter into greased 8-inch round pan. Bake 25–30 minutes, until toothpick inserted in middle of cake tests clean.

Makes 9 servings.

Calories	180	Protein	2 g
Fat	6 g	Fiber	0 g
Cholesterol	25 mg	Sodium	267 mg
Carbohydrate	29 g		

Petite Yellow Cake

Here is a nice, pleasant yellow cake.

Ingredients

2/3	cup cornstarch
2/3	cup potato starch
2	teaspoons baking powder
1/2	teaspoon salt
1	teaspoon guar gum
2/3	cup sugar
1	egg
3	tablespoons oil
1	teaspoon vanilla flavoring
1/2	teaspoon baking soda
3/4	cup milk

Directions

Preheat oven to 350°. In medium bowl, combine all ingredients except milk. While stirring, slowly add milk. Be sure all lumps are removed.

Pour batter into greased 8-inch round pan. Bake 25–30 minutes, until toothpick inserted in middle of cake tests clean.

Makes 9 servings.

Calories	189	Protein	1 g
Fat	6 g	Fiber	0 g
Cholesterol	25 mg	Sodium	325 mg
Carbohydrate	34 g		

Pound Cake

If you're looking for an elegant desert or something to share over coffee, you've come to the right spot. A few fresh berries can really dress up this cake.

Ingredients

1/3	cup softened butter
3/4	cup sugar
2	eggs
2	teaspoons vanilla flavoring
3/4	cup potato starch
3/4	cup cornstarch
1	tablespoon baking powder
3/4	teaspoon salt
1 1/4	teaspoons guar gum
3/4	cup milk

Directions

Preheat oven to 350°. In large bowl, cream together butter and sugar. Add eggs and vanilla flavoring. Mix well. Add all remaining ingredients except milk. Mix well to remove all lumps. Slowly add milk, mixing well. Batter will be thin.

Pour batter into large greased loaf pan. Bake 50 minutes, until toothpick inserted in middle of cake tests clean. Freeze extra portions.

Makes 1 large loaf. Serves 10.

Calories	215	Protein	2 g
Fat	8 g	Fiber	0 g
Cholesterol	62 mg	Sodium	344 mg
Carbohydrate	35 g		

Pineapple Upside-Down Cake

This cake is yummy—soft yellow cake under brown sugar/pineapple goodness.

For topping

- 1/2 cup brown sugar
- 1 16-ounce can pineapple slices (you will need 6 slices)
- 1 small jar maraschino cherries (optional, but nice)

Ingredients

- 2/3 cup cornstarch
- 2/3 cup potato starch
- 2 teaspoons baking powder
- 1/2 teaspoon salt
- 1 teaspoon guar gum
- 2/3 cup sugar
- 1 egg
- 3 tablespoons oil
- 1 teaspoon vanilla flavoring
- 1/2 teaspoon baking soda
- 3/4 cup milk

Directions

Preheat oven to 350°. For topping, sprinkle brown sugar on bottom of greased 8-inch round cake pan. Place 5 rings of pineapple on top of brown sugar in a circle pattern. Place remaining slice in middle. Arrange cherries in "triangle" areas where pineapple rings meet and also in center of each ring. Set aside.

For cake, in medium bowl, combine all ingredients except milk. While stirring, slowly add milk. Be sure all lumps are removed.

Pour batter atop pineapple/brown sugar in baking pan. Bake 25–30 minutes, until toothpick inserted in middle of cake tests clean. Allow to cool for a few minutes before inverting baking pan onto serving plate.

Makes 6 servings.

Calories	378	Protein	2 g
Fat	8 g	Fiber	1 g
Cholesterol	38 mg	Sodium	497 mg
Carbohydrate	75 g		

Red Velvet Cake

The original of this recipe was given to me by my grandmother. It has been presented at numerous family gatherings, from picnics to weddings. I believe this is a regional specialty, as many people have never heard of this lovely cake. It is impossible to describe its velvety texture and subtle, yet rich, flavor.

Ingredients

1/3 cup oil
1/3 cup shortening
3/4 cup plus 2 tablespoons sugar
2 eggs
2 tablespoons cocoa
1 teaspoon vanilla flavoring
1 1/4 cups buttermilk
3/4 cup potato starch
1 1/4 cups cornstarch
2 1/2 teaspoons baking powder
1/2 teaspoon salt
3 teaspoons guar gum
1 1/2 teaspoons baking soda
1 tablespoon vinegar

Directions

Preheat oven to 325°. In large bowl, combine oil, shortening, and sugar. Mix well. Add eggs, cocoa, and vanilla flavoring. Mix well. Slowly add buttermilk, mixing well. Add potato starch, cornstarch, baking powder, salt, and guar gum. Mix well. Batter will be quite thick.

In small bowl, combine baking soda and vinegar. Immediately fold into batter, incorporating well.

Pour batter into 2 greased round pans or a 9 × 13 rectangular pan. Bake 25–30 minutes, until toothpick inserted in middle of cake tests clean. Extra portions must be frozen to retain flavor and texture.

Makes 1 large cake. Serves 15.

Calories	219	Protein	2 g
Fat	11 g	Fiber	0 g
Cholesterol	29 mg	Sodium	317 mg
Carbohydrate	30 g		

Simply Sinful Chocolate Cake

My mother-in-law sent me the gluten-containing version of this recipe with a warning that "a small serving is wonderful. Too much is more than even a dedicated sweet tooth can take." I am torn between having my tastebuds delighted or confused with this cake. It is truly a flavor smorgasbord.

For bottom layer

1 cup chopped pecans
1 cup coconut

For cake

1/2 cup cocoa
1/2 cup boiling water
1 cup cornstarch
1 1/4 cups potato starch
1 tablespoon plus 1 1/2 teaspoons baking powder
1 teaspoon salt
2 teaspoons xanthan gum
1 cup sugar
2 eggs
1/4 cup oil
2 teaspoons vanilla flavoring
1 1/4 cups milk, divided

For top layer

1 8-ounce package cream cheese, softened
1/3 cup butter, softened
2 cups powdered sugar

Directions

Preheat oven to 350°. Place ingredients for bottom layer in greased 9 × 13 cake pan.

For cake, in large bowl, combine cocoa and boiling water. Mix well. Cool to room temperature. Add all other ingredients except 1 cup milk. Mix well to remove all lumps from batter. Slowly add remaining 1 cup milk. Mix well. Batter will be quite thin at first but will thicken a bit with continued mixing. Pour batter over top of pecan/coconut layer.

For top layer, combine cream cheese, butter, and powdered sugar. Mix until smooth. Place randomly over top of cake.

Bake 25–30 minutes, until toothpick inserted in middle of cake tests clean.

Makes 18 servings.

Calories	346	Protein	3 g
Fat	18 g	Fiber	2 g
Cholesterol	48 mg	Sodium	320 mg
Carbohydrate	44 g		

Spice Snacking Cake

This is the perfect "lunch box" cake. It is about half the height of a regular cake. It is moist and not too sweet.

Ingredients

1 1/3 cups cornstarch
1 1/4 cups potato starch
1 teaspoon baking powder
1 teaspoon salt
2 1/2 teaspoons guar gum
1 1/4 cups light brown sugar
2 eggs
1/4 cup oil
1 teaspoon vanilla flavoring
1 1/2 teaspoons cinnamon
3/4 teaspoon nutmeg
1/4 teaspoon cloves (optional)
1 3/4 cups milk

For topping

1/4 cup powdered sugar

Directions

Preheat oven to 350°. In medium bowl, combine all ingredients except milk. While stirring, slowly add milk. Be sure to remove all lumps. Batter will be thin.

Pour batter into greased 9 × 13 rectangular baking pan. Bake 25 minutes, until toothpick inserted into middle of cake tests clean. Cool. Top with dusting of powdered sugar.

Makes 1 large cake. Serves 15.

Calories	228	Protein	2 g
Fat	5 g	Fiber	0 g
Cholesterol	31 mg	Sodium	211 mg
Carbohydrate	44 g		

Sponge Cake

This cake is nice served with fresh berries. It tastes much like those little sponge cakes sold in stores for strawberry shortcake.

Ingredients

5 eggs, separated
3/4 cup sugar
1/4 cup water
2 teaspoons vanilla flavoring
1/2 cup cornstarch
1/3 cup potato starch
1/4 teaspoon xanthan gum
1/4 teaspoon salt
2 teaspoons baking powder
1/2 teaspoon cream of tartar

Directions

Preheat oven to 350°. Beat egg yolks until they are pale in color and they begin to thicken. Add sugar, water, and vanilla flavoring. Mix well. Add cornstarch, potato starch, xanthan gum, salt, and baking powder. Mix well, being sure to remove all lumps.

In separate bowl, beat egg whites and cream of tartar to stiff peaks. Fold egg whites into batter, incorporating well.

Pour batter into ungreased tube pan (with removable bottom). Bake 35–40 minutes, until light golden brown. Cool inverted over a glass bottle. Once cool, cut around edges of cake with knife to remove from pan.

Makes 1 large cake. Serves 12.

Calories	112	Protein	3 g
Fat	2 g	Fiber	0 g
Cholesterol	89 mg	Sodium	160 mg
Carbohydrate	21 g		

Velvet Icing

This recipe is based on one given to me by my grandmother to top Red Velvet Cake. My daughter says it is the "best." I've used this recipe on several wedding cakes. Like me, the guests loved it. My favorite cake to use this with is the Petite Chocolate Cake.

For full-sized cake

1 cup milk
2 1/2 tablespoons cornstarch
1 cup butter
1 cup sugar
2 teaspoons vanilla flavoring

For petite cake

1/2 cup milk
1 tablespoon plus 3/4 teaspoon cornstarch
1/2 cup butter
1/2 cup sugar
1 teaspoon vanilla flavoring

If you rush the preparation of this icing by not letting the milk mixture cool to room temperature, you will end up with a bowl of tasty liquid.

Directions

In microwave-safe bowl, combine milk and cornstarch. Stir well. Microwave this mixture on high for 2–4 minutes, until quite thick. Stop and stir well every minute or so. The milk and cornstarch may also be cooked in a saucepan over medium heat. Stir constantly if using this method.

Cover milk mixture with plastic wrap touching its surface. This will prevent "skin" from forming. Cool to room temperature.

In medium bowl, cream butter, sugar, and vanilla flavoring until light and fluffy. Add milk mixture and beat until frosting looks like whipped cream. This will take several minutes.

Calories	444	Protein	2 g
Fat	33 g	Fiber	0 g
Cholesterol	91 mg	Sodium	26 mg
Carbohydrate	37 g		

Yellow Cake

This is an all-purpose, traditionally textured yellow cake. It is just the kind of cake to expect at children's birthday parties.

Ingredients

1 1/3 cups cornstarch
1 1/3 cups potato starch
1 tablespoon plus 1 1/2 teaspoons baking powder
1 teaspoon salt
2 1/2 teaspoons guar gum
1 cup sugar
2 eggs
1/4 cup oil
2 teaspoons vanilla flavoring
2 cups milk, divided

Directions

Preheat oven to 350°. In large bowl, combine all ingredients except 1 cup milk. Mix well to remove all lumps from batter. Slowly add remaining 1 cup milk. Mix well.

Pour batter into two greased 8- or 9-inch round pans or into greased 9 × 13 rectangular pan. Bake 25 minutes, or until toothpick inserted in middle of cake tests clean.

Makes 1 large cake. Serves 15.

Calories	187	Protein	1 g
Fat	4 g	Fiber	0 g
Cholesterol	29 mg	Sodium	314 mg
Carbohydrate	36 g		

CHAPTER 7

Cookies

Are you ready for a special treat? This may just be my favorite chapter. I love to bake cookies and am a big cookie pusher during the holiday season.

At first I wasn't sure the unique quality of so many cookies could be duplicated gluten-free. Fortunately, they can. So many of these are so good, I couldn't pick a favorite if you asked.

As with the other recipes in this book, please use a mixer and measure carefully. It really matters.

Baking times are also very important with cookies. As the "browning" of a gluten-free cookie can be a deceptive measurement of doneness, I suggest you take one cookie off the baking sheet at the minimum baking time and test it. Tasting is, in fact, the best way to determine the baking time for your batch of cookies, as all ovens and cookie sizes are just a bit different.

Once again, note that the batters and doughs may look different, but don't let that discourage you. If you follow these recipes closely, your cookies will be attractive and tasty!

Brownies

OK, my taste-testers started getting picky on brownies. It seems some preferred their brownies more chocolaty, some liked them chewier, and some liked them cakier. Here is the ultimate compromise brownie recipe. I hope you find them to your liking.

Ingredients

1 1/3 cups sugar
1/2 cup shortening
3 eggs
2 teaspoons vanilla flavoring
1/2 cup potato starch
3/4 cup cornstarch
3/4 cup cocoa
1 teaspoon baking powder
3 teaspoons guar gum
1 cup milk
1/4 teaspoon salt

To prevent ragged edges on brownies cut them with a disposable plastic knife.

Directions

Preheat oven to 350°. In large bowl, cream sugar and shortening. Add eggs and vanilla flavoring. Mix well. Add remaining ingredients. Mix well to remove all lumps.

Spread batter into greased 9 × 13 baking pan. Bake 18–22 minutes, until toothpick inserted in middle of brownies tests clean.

Makes 15 large brownies.

Calories	212	Protein	3 g
Fat	9 g	Fiber	0 g
Cholesterol	44 mg	Sodium	94 mg
Carbohydrate	31 g		

Burnt-Edge Wafers

Do you like those burnt-edge wafers in the cookie aisle at the grocery store? I think they look so elegant. These are nearly identical in appearance—almost flat, dark at the edges, yet soft in the middle. I think these cookies taste better, too.

Ingredients

2/3 cup sugar
1/2 cup shortening
1 egg
1 teaspoon vanilla flavoring
3/4 cup potato starch
2/3 cup cornstarch
1 teaspoon baking powder
1/4 teaspoon baking soda
1/2 teaspoon xanthan gum
scant 3/4 cup milk

For topping

1 tablespoon sugar

Directions

Preheat oven to 325°. In large bowl, cream sugar and shortening. Add egg and vanilla flavoring. Mix well. Add remaining ingredients. Mix well, being sure to remove all lumps. Batter will be thin.

Drop by spoonful onto greased baking sheet. Do not tilt sheet, as batter will run. Sprinkle tops with sugar. Bake 10–12 minutes. Edges will be quite brown, and centers will be very light brown.

Makes about 3 1/2 dozen cookies.

Calories	56	Protein	0 g
Fat	3 g	Fiber	0 g
Cholesterol	5 mg	Sodium	24 mg
Carbohydrate	8 g		

Cheesecake Brownies

This recipe is perfect for anyone wanting a decadent chocolate treat. They were made for my friends Hettie (who loves cheesecake) and Bill (who loves chocolate). These brownies are so thick, so rich, and so good, Hettie and Bill both approved.

Ingredients

1 1/3 cups sugar
1/2 cup shortening
3 eggs
2 teaspoons vanilla flavoring
1/2 cup potato starch
3/4 cup cornstarch
3/4 cup cocoa
1 teaspoon baking powder
3 teaspoons guar gum
1 cup milk
1/4 teaspoon salt

For cheesecake

1 8-ounce package cream cheese
1/3 cup softened butter
2 cups powdered sugar

Directions

Preheat oven to 350°. In large bowl, cream sugar and shortening. Add eggs and vanilla flavoring. Mix well. Add remaining ingredients. Mix well to remove all lumps.

Spread batter into greased 9 × 13 cake pan. Set aside.

In medium bowl, cream together cream cheese, butter, and powdered sugar. Drop by tablespoonful onto top of brownie batter. Use knife to swirl cream cheese mixture into brownie batter.

Bake approximately 30 minutes, until toothpick inserted in middle of brownies tests clean.

Makes 15 large brownies.

Calories	353	Protein	4 g
Fat	18 g	Fiber	0 g
Cholesterol	72 mg	Sodium	139 mg
Carbohydrate	45 g		

Chocolate Chip Cookies

Try one of these right out of the oven. It is truly love at first bite. I will not tell you that these taste exactly like traditional chocolate chip cookies, but they're real close.

Ingredients

1/4 cup softened butter
1/4 cup oil
3/4 cup dark brown sugar
2 egg yolks
1 teaspoon vanilla flavoring
1/3 cup water
1/2 teaspoon of xanthan gum
3/4 cup potato starch
1/2 cup cornstarch
1/4 teaspoon baking soda
1/2 teaspoon salt
1 1/4 cups semisweet chocolate chips

Directions

Preheat oven to 350°. In large bowl, cream butter, oil, and brown sugar. Add egg yolks, vanilla flavoring, and water. Mix well. Add remaining ingredients except for chocolate chips. Mix well, being sure to remove all lumps. Fold in chocolate chips.

Drop by rounded teaspoonful onto greased baking sheets. Bake 8–10 minutes.

Makes 3 1/2 to 4 dozen cookies.

NOTE: These cookies will soften if stored in an airtight container. Freeze your extras, or allow them some air for a few minutes before serving.

Calories	71	Protein	0 g
Fat	4 g	Fiber	0 g
Cholesterol	12 mg	Sodium	32 mg
Carbohydrate	9 g		

Chocolate Drops

You might like to use these plain cookies for a Cookie Crumb Crust. Or even sandwich them with a little cream cheese blended with powdered sugar. Or, you might just like to eat them. They are not very sweet, quite chocolatey, and a little crisp.

Ingredients

1/4 cup shortening
3/4 cup sugar
1/4 cup oil
2 teaspoons vanilla flavoring
2 eggs
1/2 cup cocoa
1/2 cup potato starch
3/4 cup cornstarch
1/2 teaspoon guar gum
1/2 teaspoon xanthan gum
3/4 teaspoon salt
1/4 cup water

For tops

1 tablespoon sugar

Directions

Preheat oven to 350°. In medium bowl, cream together shortening, sugar, and oil. Add remaining ingredients. Mix well to remove all lumps.

Drop by small teaspoonful onto greased baking sheet. For perfect rounds, use a pastry bag and round tube to place batter onto sheet. Place a pinch of sugar on top of each cookie. Bake 10 minutes, until lightly browned at edges. If your cookies don't seem crisp enough, bake them a minute or two longer.

Makes 5–8 dozen depending on size.

Calories	27	Protein	0 g
Fat	1 g	Fiber	0 g
Cholesterol	4 mg	Sodium	18 mg
Carbohydrate	3 g		

Crispy Sugar Cookies

My youngest son called these "Crunchy, Crunchy, Crisp." They're really not that crunchy, but they are crisp, light, and flavorful. They were included in our "regular food" holiday cookie tray, and no one could tell that they were "different."

Ingredients

1 cup shortening
3/4 cup sugar
3/4 cup light brown sugar
2 eggs
1 teaspoon vanilla flavoring
1 cup potato starch
1 3/4 cups corn starch
1 teaspoon baking soda
1 tablespoon baking powder
4 teaspoons guar gum
1 teaspoon salt

Directions

Preheat oven to 350°. In large bowl, cream together shortening, sugar, and light brown sugar. Add eggs and vanilla flavoring. Mix well. Add remaining ingredients. Mix well to remove all lumps.

Drop by teaspoonful onto greased baking sheet. Bake 9–10 minutes or until lightly browned. Cool briefly on baking sheet. Store in airtight container.

Makes about 4 dozen cookies.

Calories	95	Protein	0 g
Fat	5 g	Fiber	0 g
Cholesterol	9 mg	Sodium	109 mg
Carbohydrate	14 g		

Pecan Meringues

This cookie is a cousin to Hazelnut Balls. The pecans and vanilla blend well for an understated richness in this simple cookie.

Ingredients

2 egg whites

1 teaspoon vanilla flavoring

1/4 teaspoon cream of tartar

1 cup sugar

1 1/2 cups ground pecans

Directions

Preheat oven to 300°. In large bowl, beat egg whites, vanilla flavoring, and cream of tartar until frothy. Continue beating while gradually adding sugar. Beat until stiff peaks form. Fold in ground pecans.

Drop by rounded teaspoonful onto greased baking sheet. Bake 25 minutes. Cool on wire rack.

Makes about 4 dozen cookies.

Calories	40	Protein	0 g
Fat	2 g	Fiber	0 g
Cholesterol	0 mg	Sodium	2 mg
Carbohydrate	5 g		

Double Chocolate Cookies

These cookies are chocolaty. If you have kids, please let them try one fresh from the oven. They're a real treat.

Ingredients

1/4 cup softened butter
3/4 cup dark brown sugar
2 egg yolks
1 teaspoon vanilla flavoring
1/3 cup water
1/4 cup oil
1/2 cup potato starch
1/2 cup cornstarch
1/4 cup cocoa
1/4 teaspoon baking soda
1/2 teaspoon xanthan gum
1/2 teaspoon salt
1 1/4 cups semisweet chocolate chips

Directions

Preheat oven to 350°. In large bowl, cream together butter and brown sugar. Add egg yolks, vanilla flavoring, water, and oil. Mix well. Add remaining ingredients except for chocolate chips. Mix well, being sure to remove all lumps. Fold in chocolate chips.

Drop by rounded teaspoonful onto greased baking sheet. Bake 8–10 minutes.

Makes 3 1/2–4 dozen cookies.

NOTE: These cookies will soften if stored in an airtight container. Freeze your extras, or give them a few minutes of air before serving.

Calories	70	Protein	0 g
Fat	4 g	Fiber	0 g
Cholesterol	12 mg	Sodium	32 mg
Carbohydrate	9 g		

Gingersnaps

This cookie was fashioned after the gingersnaps that I used to make for my grandfather. They are crisp on the outside with a very slight, soft chewiness at the center. This is a great dough. Roll them out for gingerbread men if you like.

Ingredients

1/4 cup shortening
1/2 cup sugar
1/3 cup molasses
2 egg yolks
1 1/4 cups cornstarch
3/4 cup potato starch
1/2 teaspoon baking soda
1/4 cup oil
1 teaspoon xanthan gum
1/2 teaspoon salt
1 1/2 teaspoons ground ginger
1/4 teaspoon cinnamon

For topping

1 tablespoon sugar

Directions

Preheat oven to 350°. In large bowl, cream together shortening, sugar, and molasses. Add remaining ingredients, mixing well to remove all lumps.

Drop by rounded teaspoonful onto greased baking sheet. Sprinkle well with sugar. Bake 8–9 minutes. Dough will be just set, with no wet spot in the middle. Overbaking will make these cookies too hard and a tad bitter.

Makes about 3 dozen cookies.

Calories	75	Protein	0 g
Fat	3 g	Fiber	0 g
Cholesterol	12 mg	Sodium	51 mg
Carbohydrate	11 g		

Ladyfingers

These delicate cookies are so light that you feel like you're barely eating anything. These little wisps of sponge cake are tasty; it's hard to eat only one.

Ingredients

2	eggs, separated
1/8	teaspoon cream of tartar
	pinch of salt
1/4	teaspoon vanilla flavoring
1/4	cup sugar
2	tablespoons cornstarch
2	tablespoons potato starch
1/8	teaspoon guar gum
1/2	teaspoon water

For topping

1	tablespoon powdered sugar

Directions

Preheat oven to 325°. In medium bowl, beat egg whites and cream of tartar to stiff peaks. Set aside.

In medium bowl, mix all remaining ingredients until pale yellow. Fold in egg whites.

Spoon about one tablespoon of batter into 3 1/2 inch long "finger" on greased baking sheet. Batter will spread to about 3/4 inch wide. Bake 8–10 minutes until browned at edges and sponge is firm.

Allow to cool briefly before removing from baking sheet. These cookies will stick, requiring additional care in removing from baking sheet.

Sprinkle tops of cookies with powdered sugar.

Makes about 2 1/2 dozen lady fingers.

Calories	16	Protein	0 g
Fat	0 g	Fiber	0 g
Cholesterol	14 mg	Sodium	9 mg
Carbohydrate	3 g		

Lemon Cookie Bars

It was difficult to decide whether to make a big pan of these cookies or a small pan of these cookies. My tastebuds said big. Reality said small. These are very rich, so cut the servings small.

For 1st layer

1/2 cup shortening
3/4 cup sugar
1/2 cup potato starch
3/4 cup cornstarch
2 teaspoons baking powder
1/2 teaspoon salt
1 1/2 teaspoons xanthan gum
1/4 cup milk

For 2nd layer

1 1/4 cups water
1/4 cup lemon juice
2 egg yolks
2/3 cup sugar
4 tablespoons cornstarch

For top

1 tablespoon powdered sugar

Directions

Preheat oven to 375°. In medium bowl, combine all 1st layer ingredients. Mix until mixture becomes a soft dough and all lumps are removed.

Press into bottom of greased 8 × 8 or 9 × 9 pan. Bake 20–25 minutes, until top is browned. Set aside.

In medium saucepan, combine all 2nd layer ingredients. Mix well and cook over medium heat until mixture thickens. Immediately pour on top of 1st layer. Allow to cool.

Dust top of 2nd layer with powdered sugar, as desired.

Makes 9 servings.

Calories	320	Protein	1 g
Fat	13 g	Fiber	1 g
Cholesterol	49 mg	Sodium	245 mg
Carbohydrate	52 g		

Lemon Sugar Cookies

These cakelike cookies remind me of some my mom used to make—slightly crisp on the outside, soft and tender on the inside. Mom's were lemon, so mine are too. Substitute vanilla flavoring if you prefer.

Ingredients

1/2 cup shortening
2/3 cup sugar
1 egg
1 teaspoon lemon flavoring
3/4 cup potato starch
2/3 cup cornstarch
1 teaspoon baking powder
3/4 teaspoon xanthan gum
1/4 teaspoon baking soda
1/2 teaspoon salt
scant 3/4 cup milk

For topping

1 tablespoon sugar

Directions

Preheat oven to 350°. In large bowl, cream together shortening and sugar. Add egg and lemon flavoring. Mix well. Add remaining ingredients except milk. Slowly add milk while mixing. Mix well to remove all lumps.

Drop by rounded teaspoonful onto greased baking sheet. Bake 8–10 minutes, until edges are lightly browned. Sprinkle tops with sugar.

Makes about 3 1/2 dozen cookies.

Calories	56	Protein	0 g
Fat	3 g	Fiber	0 g
Cholesterol	5 mg	Sodium	50 mg
Carbohydrate	8 g		

Peanut Butter Cookies

Here is an easy, tasty peanut butter cookie recipe. I personally like to toss in a few semisweet chocolate chips when I make these cookies, but they're quite tasty with no chips.

Ingredients

2 tablespoons shortening
1/3 cup peanut butter
1/4 cup sugar
1/2 cup brown sugar
1/4 cup oil
1 egg
3/4 cup potato starch
3/4 cup cornstarch
1 teaspoon xanthan gum
1/2 teaspoon salt
2 tablespoons water
(There is no baking powder or baking soda in this recipe.)

Directions

Preheat oven to 350°. In medium bowl, combine all ingredients. Mix well.

Shape a slightly rounded teaspoonful of dough into a small ball. Place on an ungreased baking sheet. Press tops of each cookie with tines of a fork to create traditional grid pattern.

Bake approximately 9 minutes, until tops of cookies are no longer shiny and bottoms are lightly browned.

Makes about 3 dozen cookies.

Calories	76	Protein	1 g
Fat	4 g	Fiber	0 g
Cholesterol	6 mg	Sodium	45 mg
Carbohydrate	10 g		

Raisin Spice Cookies

These poofy cookies seem light at first, then flavorful, and finally quite satisfying. Quite a pleasant cookie.

Ingredients

1/4 cup shortening
2/3 cup light brown sugar
1 egg
1/4 cup oil
1 teaspoon vanilla flavoring
3/4 teaspoon cinnamon
1/4 teaspoon nutmeg
3/4 cup potato starch
2/3 cup cornstarch
1/2 teaspoon baking soda
1/2 teaspoon salt
3/4 teaspoon xanthan gum
1/2 cup milk
1 1/4 cups raisins

Directions

Preheat oven to 350°. In large bowl, cream together shortening and light brown sugar. Add egg, oil, vanilla flavoring, cinnamon, and nutmeg. Mix well. Add potato starch, cornstarch, baking soda, salt, and xanthan gum. While mixing, slowly add milk, being sure to remove all lumps. Fold in raisins.

Drop by rounded teaspoonful onto greased baking sheet. Bake 9–10 minutes, until very lightly browned.

Makes about 3 1/2 dozen cookies.

Calories	70	Protein	0 g
Fat	3 g	Fiber	0 g
Cholesterol	5 mg	Sodium	46 mg
Carbohydrate	11 g		

Rolled Sugar Cookies

This is a wonderful dough to work with. And the cookies are crisp outside, tender inside. If you like making cookies for special holidays, this is a must-try recipe.

Ingredients

1/4 cup shortening
2/3 cup sugar
1/4 cup oil
2 egg yolks
1 1/2 teaspoons vanilla flavoring
3/4 cup potato starch
1 cup cornstarch
1 teaspoon xanthan gum
1/2 teaspoon salt
2 tablespoons water
(There is no baking powder or baking soda in this recipe.)

Directions

Preheat oven to 350°. In large bowl, cream together shortening, sugar, and oil. Add egg yolks and vanilla flavoring. Mix well. Add remaining ingredients. Mix well to remove any lumps.

Lightly "flour" surface and rolling pin with cornstarch. Roll out dough to 1/8 inch thickness and use cookie cutters to cut out the dough into desired shapes.

For easier handling, especially on a hot or humid day, consider placing this dough in the refrigerator for a few hours.

Place cookies on greased baking sheet. Decorate with colored sugar or sprinkles as desired. Bake 8–10 minutes. These cookies will just begin to brown around the bottom.

Makes about 3 dozen cookies.

Calories	68	Protein	0 g
Fat	3 g	Fiber	0 g
Cholesterol	12 mg	Sodium	31 mg
Carbohydrate	10 g		

Shortbread Cookies

No matter how many shortbread recipes you've seen that call for rice flour, it is absolutely not needed, or even desirable, to produce these rich, buttery cookies. I must tell you that these cookies were loved by almost all of my testers but hated by a few. There was no middle ground on this cookie.

Ingredients

1/3 cup softened butter
3/4 cup powdered sugar
1/4 cup oil
3/4 cup potato starch
1 1/4 cups cornstarch
1 teaspoon xanthan gum
1/2 teaspoon salt
3 tablespoons cream
1/4 teaspoon vanilla flavoring (optional)

Directions

Preheat oven to 325°. In large bowl, cream together butter and powdered sugar. Add remaining ingredients. Mix well, being sure to remove all lumps. Roll out this moist, soft dough on "floured"—with cornstarch—surface to about 1/4 inch thickness. Cut dough into desired shapes and prick with a fork if traditional shortbread look is desired.

Use spatula to lift cookies from floured surface to greased baking sheet. Bake 18–20 minutes, until just the slightest hint of browning occurs.

Makes 25–30 1½-inch round cookies.

Calories	84	Protein	0 g
Fat	5 g	Fiber	0 g
Cholesterol	8 mg	Sodium	38 mg
Carbohydrate	11 g		

Snickerdoodles

My nonceliac taste testers are often not told that they are testing gluten-free foods. The tray holding these cookies was returned empty with an inquiry of where to get some more. I'm sure you'll enjoy this crackled-top cookie as much as the testers did.

Ingredients

1/2 cup shortening
3/4 cup sugar
1 egg
1 teaspoon vanilla flavoring
1/2 cup potato starch
3/4 cup plus 2 tablespoons cornstarch
1/4 teaspoon baking soda
1 teaspoon baking powder
1 teaspoon xanthan gum
1/2 teaspoon salt
2 tablespoons water

For cinnamon/sugar mixture

2 tablespoons sugar
1/2 teaspoon cinnamon

Directions

Preheat oven to 350°. In a large bowl, cream together shortening and sugar. Add egg and vanilla flavoring. Mix well. Add potato starch, cornstarch, baking soda, baking powder, xanthan gum, salt, and water. Mix well to eliminate any lumps. Dough will be sticky.

Lightly oil hands or spray them with nonstick spray to better handle dough. Shape into small balls, using a slightly rounded teaspoonful of dough for each cookie. Roll in sugar/cinnamon mixture.

Place on lightly greased baking sheet and press each ball to even thickness of about 1/3 inch. Bake 10–12 minutes. A single cookie should be removed at the shortest baking time to test for doneness. Browning is not a good indicator for these cookies.

Makes about 3 dozen cookies.

Calories	65	Protein	0 g
Fat	3 g	Fiber	0 g
Cholesterol	6 mg	Sodium	55 mg
Carbohydrate	9 g		

Spritz

This recipe requires use of a pastry bag or cookie press to shape the cookies. Spritz cookies are included every year on our holiday cookie plate. The piped edges on these cookies are not as pronounced as their wheat-containing counterparts. I sacrificed a bit on appearance to save taste and texture. These are my daughter's favorite. She insisted that they be included in this book, describing them as "awesome!"

Ingredients

1/4	cup shortening
1	cup sugar
1/4	cup oil
2	eggs
1 1/2	teaspoons vanilla flavoring
3/4	cup potato starch
1	cup cornstarch
1 1/8	teaspoons xanthan gum
1	teaspoon salt
1/4	cup cream

Directions

Preheat oven to 350°. In medium bowl, cream together the shortening, sugar, and oil. Add remaining ingredients and mix well to remove all lumps.

Pipe or press dough onto greased baking sheet in desired shapes. I often make the traditional "S" shape using a star tip (#21). Bake 7–8 minutes, until base of cookie just begins to brown.

Makes approximately 6 dozen cookies.

Calories	40	Protein	0 g
Fat	2 g	Fiber	0 g
Cholesterol	7 mg	Sodium	32 mg
Carbohydrate	6 g		

Toffee Bars

This cookie bar is quick to make. It is also quick to disappear, as it has everything going for it—chocolate, nuts, and toffee.

For 1st layer

1/4 cup shortening
1/3 cup plus 1 tablespoon brown sugar
1/4 cup potato starch
1/3 cup cornstarch
1 teaspoons baking powder
1/4 teaspoon salt
3/4 teaspoon xanthan gum
2 tablespoons milk

For 2nd layer

3/4 cup semisweet chocolate chips

For topping

1/2 cup finely chopped pecans

Directions

Preheat oven to 375°. In medium bowl, combine all 1st layer ingredients. Mix until mixture becomes a soft dough and all lumps are removed.

Press into bottom of greased 8 × 8 or 9 × 9 pan. Bake 12–15 minutes, until dough is thoroughly set.

Immediately place chocolate chips on top of hot cookie bar layer. Cover pan with foil until chips are melted. Spread once chocolate softens.

Sprinkle chopped pecans on top of melted chocolate. Cool.

Makes 18 small bars.

Calories	119	Protein	1 g
Fat	8 g	Fiber	1 g
Cholesterol	0 mg	Sodium	64 mg
Carbohydrate	14 g		

Vanilla Wafers

These little cookies are just a little higher and paler in color than store-bought vanilla wafers. But they taste better than the store-bought version, too. Seems like a good trade-off to me!

Ingredients

1/4 cup shortening
3/4 cup sugar
1/4 cup oil
2 teaspoons vanilla flavoring
2 eggs
3/4 cup potato starch
1 cup cornstarch
1/2 teaspoon guar gum
1/2 teaspoon xanthan gum
3/4 teaspoon salt
1/4 cup water

Directions

Preheat oven to 350°. In medium bowl, cream together shortening, sugar, and oil. Add remaining ingredients. Mix well to remove all lumps.

Drop by small teaspoonful onto greased baking sheet. For perfect rounds, use a pastry bag and round tube to place batter onto sheet. Bake 10 minutes, until lightly browned at edges. If your cookies don't seem crisp enough, bake a minute or two longer.

Makes 7–8 dozen small cookies.

Calories	27	Protein	0 g
Fat	1 g	Fiber	0 g
Cholesterol	4 mg	Sodium	18 mg
Carbohydrate	4 g		

CHAPTER 8

Pies and Tarts

A good-tasting piecrust is impossible gluten-free, you think? Well, I'm here to tell that you you're wrong! This book has a really good traditional piecrust—really! The dough is a bit harder to handle than its wheat-containing counterpart, but it's worth the effort.

And if you have a dozen or so gluten-free cookies on hand, you can always make a quick Cookie Crumb Crust. Either way, pies are a sure winner.

I'm very opinionated about pie fillings, too. I've never believed that a small amount of filling should be put into a pie when someone has gone to the trouble of making a crust from scratch. Many of these recipes use 50 percent more filling than regular recipes. The fillings are too much for those almost-flat disposable aluminum pie plates, so don't use them. You'll need to use a real one. And enjoy!

The tarts are a quick and easy way to make an elegant dessert. They taste good, too.

Apple Pie

This is a traditional apple pie with a lattice top. The juices from the apples are not overly thickened.

Recommended crust

2 batches of Traditional Piecrust (page 232)

Ingredients

1/4 cup sugar (use a bit more if using tart apples)

2 1/2 tablespoons cornstarch

5 large apples (6 cups), peeled, cored, sliced

Directions

Prepare piecrust recipe. Halve dough in two equal portions. With one portion, roll dough between two pieces of waxed paper (or on a "floured"—with cornstarch—tabletop) into a large circle. This must be large enough to fill a 9-inch pie pan with a bit over the sides. Remove top piece of waxed paper and flip crust into pie pan.

Cover with a damp towel and set aside. Cover unused dough and set aside as well.

Preheat oven to 400°. In small bowl, combine sugar and cornstarch. Mix well. Set aside.

In large bowl, combine apples and sugar mixture. Toss well, but be gentle with the apples. Pour apple mixture into pie pan.

Roll out remaining dough as before. Cut into 1-inch strips (right through the waxed paper is fine). Lay across top of pie. Weave layers to form lattice, removing waxed paper as you go.

Bake 10 minutes. Reduce heat to 350° and bake 35–40 more minutes. Crust will be nicely browned and apples soft when pierced with a fork.

Serves 6.

Calories	652	Protein	1 g
Fat	36 g	Fiber	11 g
Cholesterol	2 mg	Sodium	390 mg
Carbohydrate	85 g		

Blueberry Tart

I wanted to prepare something wonderful with blueberries, but not quite as robust as a blueberry pie. This tart uses a freshly baked piecrust for the base, and the filling is cooked on top of the stove. And finally, it's topped off with fresh whipped cream. It should be a real hit during blueberry season.

Recommended crust

Traditional Piecrust (baked in bottom only of spring form pan and cooled), (page 232) *or*

Cookie Crumb Crust (prepared in a springform pan), (page 217)

For filling

1 pint (2 cups) blueberries, fresh or frozen

1/3 cup water

1/4 cup sugar

1 tablespoon cornstarch

Recommended topping

Whipped Cream (page 264)

Directions

Prepare piecrust as desired. Set aside.

In small saucepan, combine all ingredients for filling. Mix well, being careful not to crush the berries. Cook until thickened. Pour filling on top of prepared piecrust. Refrigerate.

Shortly before serving, prepare Whipped Cream. Cut individual servings of tart and top with Whipped Cream as desired.

Makes 8 servings.

Calories	358	Protein	1 g
Fat	24 g	Fiber	4 g
Cholesterol	43 mg	Sodium	161 mg
Carbohydrate	35 g		

Cherry Pie

This is a traditional Cherry Pie with a full-top crust. If you serve it with ice cream, I'll be right over!

Recommended crust

2 batches of Traditional Piecrust (page 232)

Ingredients

$1\frac{1}{2}$ quarts sour cherries, pitted

$1\frac{1}{4}$ cups sugar (use less sugar for sweet cherries)

6 tablespoons cornstarch

Directions

Prepare piecrust recipe. Halve dough in two equal portions. With one portion, roll dough between two pieces of waxed paper (or on a "floured"—with cornstarch—tabletop) into a large circle. This must be large enough to fill a 9-inch pie pan with a bit over the sides. Remove top piece of waxed paper and flip crust into pie pan.

When sour cherries are in season, consider preparing some extras for use out of season. Simply wash, pit, and freeze.

Cover with a damp towel and set aside. Cover unused dough and set aside as well.

Preheat oven to 400°. In medium saucepan, combine all ingredients. Stir well but gently. Cook until mixture thickens. Pour the cherry mixture into pie pan.

Roll out remaining dough as before, placing piecrust on top of pie. Cut off excess dough. Pinch dough around edge of piecrust to form an attractive border. Cut a few air vents in top of piecrust.

Place pie on top of a baking sheet as a few of the juices may escape the pie while baking.

Bake 10 minutes. Reduce heat to 350° and bake 35–40 more minutes. Crust will be nicely browned and juices translucent.

Serves 6.

Calories	795	Protein	3 g
Fat	36 g	Fiber	11 g
Cholesterol	2 mg	Sodium	395 mg
Carbohydrate	121 g		

Chocolate Meringue Pie

Chocolate Meringue Pie is my favorite. If you prefer Whipped Cream on top of your pie, just substitute it for the Meringue. This pie is delicious either way.

Recommended crust

Traditional Piecrust (page 232) *or*
Cookie Crumb Crust (baked and cooled), (page 217)

For filling

3 cups milk
2 1/2 teaspoons vanilla flavoring
3/4 cup sugar
4 1/2 tablespoons cornstarch
1/3 cup cocoa
1 egg

Recommended topping

1 recipe Meringue (freshly made), (page 251)

Directions

Prepare piecrust. Bake as directed. Set aside.

In medium saucepan, combine all ingredients for filling. Stir well to blend. Cocoa will float on top of milk but will incorporate while warming. Over medium heat, stir constantly until mixture beings to thicken and boil. Remove from heat and pour into prepared piecrust. Set aside.

Prepare meringue. Spread meringue over top of the pudding and to the very edges of the piecrust. This will help prevent the meringue from shrinking. Use the back of a spoon to create decorative swirls or peaks in the meringue.

Place pie under broiler (low heat) for a few minutes to brown meringue. Refrigerate before serving.

Makes 6 servings.

Calories	530	Protein	8 g
Fat	21 g	Fiber	4 g
Cholesterol	46 mg	Sodium	295 mg
Carbohydrate	76 g		

Apple Tart

This is an elegant, understated tart. It is not "hearty," rather a light finish to a meal.

Recommended crust

Sweet Pastry Crust (prepared, but not baked), (page 234)

Ingredients

3 apples (peeled, cored, cut into small wedges)
1 tablespoon sugar
1/4 teaspoon cinnamon (optional)

Directions

Prepare Sweet Pastry Crust. Press crust into bottom of greased 9-inch springform (or tart) pan.

Preheat oven to 350°. Prepare apples and place in attractive pattern in pan. Sprinkle sugar atop apples. Sprinkle cinnamon on top as well, if desired.

Bake 35 minutes until lightly browned.

Makes 6 servings.

Calories	244	Protein	1 g
Fat	10 g	Fiber	2 g
Cholesterol	36 mg	Sodium	92 mg
Carbohydrate	39 g		

Cookie Crumb Crust

This crust is quick and easy to make. It's extra-tasty made with homemade cookies, but any ready-made cookies should work well, too. Be sure to choose a cookie that compliments the flavor of your pie filling. This crust is especially nice to use to prepare a quick dessert—with pudding or softened ice cream.

Ingredients

1 1/4 cups finely crushed cookie crumbs (about 10–12 medium-sized cookies)

1/4 cup melted butter

Directions

Combine all ingredients in bottom of pie pan. Mix well. Press mixture onto sides and bottom of pan. Try to press it to an even thickness. Allow to cool. Do not bake. Fill as desired.

Calories	155	Protein	0 g
Fat	12 g	Fiber	0 g
Cholesterol	22 mg	Sodium	1 mg
Carbohydrate	12 g		

The easiest way I know to make cookie crumbs is to place 5–6 cookies in a zipped-top plastic bag, remove the air, and roll with a rolling pin.

Custard Pie

This was my granddad's favorite pie. He loved this and cornstarch pudding. I hope you enjoy it, too.

Recommended crust

Traditional Piecrust (page 232)

Ingredients

5 eggs
1/3 cup sugar
1 teaspoon vanilla flavoring
2 cups milk
few pinches of nutmeg

Directions

Make piecrust. Do not bake. Set aside.

Preheat oven to 400°. In medium bowl, combine eggs and sugar. Stir until eggs are fully mixed. Add vanilla flavoring and milk. Again, mix until eggs are fully incorporated. Pour into prepared piecrust. Dust with nutmeg as desired.

Bake 10 minutes. Reduce heat to 325°. Bake an additional 45 minutes, until knife inserted in middle of custard tests clean.

Makes 6 servings.

Calories	413	Protein	8 g
Fat	23 g	Fiber	4 g
Cholesterol	185 mg	Sodium	288 mg
Carbohydrate	43 g		

Pumpkin Pie

I personally like pies with lots of filling, and this one fills a 9-inch pie plate. This pie is not too spicy, not too mild. It is a crowd pleaser.

Recommended crust

Traditional Piecrust (page 232)

Ingredients

1 15- to 16-ounce can pumpkin
1 12-ounce can evaporated milk
3/4 cup light brown sugar
1/2 teaspoon salt
1 teaspoon cinnamon
1/4 teaspoon ginger
1/4 teaspoon nutmeg
2 eggs

Directions

Preheat oven to 400°. Prepare 9-inch piecrust and set aside. Do not bake.

In medium bowl, combine all ingredients. Mix well to remove any lumps. Pour batter into prepared piecrust.

Bake 15 minutes. Reduce heat to 350°. Bake an additional 45–50 minutes, until knife inserted in middle of pie tests clean. The filling will appear puffy.

Makes 6 servings.

Calories	506	Protein	7 g
Fat	24 g	Fiber	6 g
Cholesterol	89 mg	Sodium	469 mg
Carbohydrate	68 g		

Key Lime Pie

Unless you live in Florida, key limes will be hard to come by, although you may come across key lime juice in some grocery stores and many gourmet stores. If you do have access to this juice, substitute it for both the lemon and lime juices used in this recipe. In good conscience, I couldn't give you a recipe using uncooked eggs (as is the case in many recipes for this pie). The filling for this pie is cooked in a saucepan in just a few minutes to avoid possible exposure to raw eggs.

Recommended crust

Cookie Crumb Crust (page 217)

For filling

1 12-ounce can evaporated milk
1 1/3 cups sugar
4 eggs
scant 1/4 cup lemon juice
1/2 cup lime juice
5 tablespoons cornstarch
4 drops green food coloring (optional)

Recommended topping

Whipped Cream (freshly made), (page 264)

If you're using real key lime juice, increase the cornstarch to 7 tablespoons. The higher acidity of this juice lessens the gelling ability of the cornstarch. Real key lime juice makes for a tarter pie—as it should be.

Directions

Prepare piecrust. Set aside.

In medium saucepan, combine all ingredients for filling. Mix well. Over medium heat, stir constantly until mixture beings to thicken and boil. Remove from heat and immediately pour into prepared piecrust. Refrigerate.

Prepare Whipped Cream. Serve with pie.

Makes 6 servings.

Calories	622	Protein	9 g
Fat	34 g	Fiber	0 g
Cholesterol	237 mg	Sodium	120 mg
Carbohydrate	73 g		

Lemon Meringue Pie

This Lemon Meringue Pie is a little tart and not too sweet, which just happens to be the way I like it. When you make the meringue, remember to omit the vanilla flavoring.

Recommended crust

Traditional Piecrust (baked and cooled)

For filling

2 1/2 cups water
1/2 cup lemon juice
3 egg yolks
1 1/3 cups sugar
8 tablespoons cornstarch

Recommended topping

1 recipe Meringue—but omit vanilla flavoring (freshly made), (page 251)

Directions

Prepare piecrust. Bake as directed. Set aside.

In medium saucepan, combine all ingredients for filling. Stir well to blend. Over medium heat, stir constantly until mixture beings to thicken and boil. Remove from heat and pour into prepared piecrust. Set aside.

Prepare meringue. Spread meringue over top of the filling and to the very edges of the piecrust. This will help prevent the meringue from shrinking. Use the back of a spoon to create decorative swirls or peaks in the meringue.

Place pie under broiler (on low) for a few minutes to brown meringue. Refrigerate.

Makes 6 servings.

Calories	436	Protein	4 g
Fat	20 g	Fiber	4 g
Cholesterol	110 mg	Sodium	230 mg
Carbohydrate	61 g		

Peach Streusel Pie

Peach pie is now served more often in our home since this one came out of the oven. My children wouldn't let it be taken out the door. I know that nutmeg is traditionally paired with peaches, but I think cinnamon is especially nice.

Recommended crust

Traditional Piecrust (page 232)

Ingredients

5–6 large peaches, pitted, peeled, and sliced (about 6 cups)
1/3 cup sugar
1/2 teaspoon cinnamon
3 tablespoons cornstarch

Topping

1 recipe Streusel (page 262)

Directions

Prepare traditional piecrust. Do not bake. Set aside.

Preheat oven to 400°. Prepare peaches, set aside. In small bowl, combine sugar, cinnamon, and cornstarch. Pour sugar mixture over sliced peaches and mix very well, but avoid crushing fruit. Pour peach mixture into prepared piecrust.

Prepare Streusel and place atop pie.

Bake 15 minutes. Turn heat down to 350°. Bake an additional 35–45 minutes. All of the Streusel will be fully cooked (no wet spots), and any visible juices will be thickened.

Makes 6 servings.

Calories	714	Protein	2 g
Fat	35 g	Fiber	8 g
Cholesterol	2 mg	Sodium	558 mg
Carbohydrate	102 g		

Pecan Pie

I've never been a huge fan of pecan pie. It seemed just a tad too gooey and a tad too sweet. In this recipe, I've retained all the richness and flavor of regular pecan pie but cut down on the sweetness and firmed up the gooey part. I've also increased the amount of filling just a little to accommodate my belief that a piecrust should not be half full. I am now a big fan of pecan pie.

Recommended crust

Traditional Piecrust (prepared, but not baked), (page 232)

For filling

4 eggs
1 1/4 cups brown sugar
3/4 teaspoon salt
1 cup light corn syrup
1 1/2 teaspoons vanilla flavoring
1/2 teaspoon vinegar
1 1/4 cups pecan halves

Directions

Preheat oven to 400°. Prepare piecrust. Do not bake. Set aside.

Combine eggs, brown sugar, salt, melted butter, corn syrup, vanilla flavoring, and vinegar. Mix well to remove all lumps and fully incorporate eggs. Stir in pecans. Pour mixture into prepared piecrust.

Bake 15 minutes. Turn heat down to 350° and bake approximately 50 more minutes. A knife inserted in the middle of the pie will test clean.

Because this pie is quite rich, it serves 8 easily.

Calories	649	Protein	5 g
Fat	32 g	Fiber	5 g
Cholesterol	107 mg	Sodium	440 mg
Carbohydrate	91 g		

Strawberry Pie

We have a small strawberry patch at our home. My kids ran into the kitchen with piles of strawberries one beautiful Sunday morning and said, "Make a pie for your book, Mom." I thought, "What wonderful children! Good idea!" Unfortunately, they started eating the strawberries. Needless to say, they all disappeared. I was forced to wait for more berries to ripen. I picked the berries for this pie while the kids were in school. I've combined my preference for strawberries and custard sauce by using a custard base in place of the traditional cream cheese base. I hope you like it.

Recommended crust

Traditional Piecrust (prepared, baked, and cooled), (page 232)

For 1st layer of filling

1 cup milk
3 eggs
1/4 cup sugar
1/2 teaspoon vanilla flavoring
1 tablespoon cornstarch

For 2nd layer of filling

3 cups fresh strawberries, washed and hulled

For 3rd layer of filling

1 cup fresh strawberries, smashed or pureed
3/4 cup water
2 tablespoons cornstarch
2 tablespoons sugar

Recommended topping (optional)

Whipped Cream (page 264)

This pie is pictured on the cover, made with the traditional piecrust as suggested.

Directions

Prepare piecrust. Bake and cool.

In medium saucepan, cream together ingredients for 1st layer. Heat over medium heat until mixture begins to thicken, stirring constantly to avoid curdling. Spread evenly on bottom of piecrust. Allow to cool to room temperature. Arrange fresh whole strawberries, tops down, in pleasing manner on top of 1st layer. Set aside.

In small saucepan, combine ingredients for 3rd layer. Stir well. Cook over medium heat until mixture thickens. Spoon evenly over berries. Refrigerate for at least 2 hours to chill.

Top with fresh Whipped Cream before serving, if desired.

Makes 6 servings.

Calories	418	Protein	6 g
Fat	21 g	Fiber	6 g
Cholesterol	111 mg	Sodium	249 mg
Carbohydrate	52 g		

Turnovers

Turnovers are really just little folded pies packaged to go. Because each turnover contains such a small amount of filling, it is very important that very flavorful fruit be used. Otherwise, the flavor gets lost in the crust. Substitute frozen fruit before buying fruit out of season.

Recommended crust

Traditional Piecrust (dough prepared but not baked), (page 232)

For filling

1 1/2–2	cups fresh or frozen peaches (peeled, pitted, and sliced), blueberries, or sour cherries
2	tablespoons sugar
1	tablespoon cornstarch

Topping

1/4	cup powdered sugar
	few drops of vanilla flavoring
2	teaspoons milk or water

Directions

Prepare piecrust dough; set aside.

Preheat oven to 375°. For filling, combine all ingredients in small bowl. Set aside.

Roll out half of dough between two sheets of waxed paper. Remove top piece of waxed paper. Cut 5-inch squares from the dough. Place approximately 1 tablespoon of filling into center of square. While leaving waxed paper on the downside of the dough, fold dough over filling to form a triangle. Slowly remove waxed paper and press edges of dough together to seal.

Place turnover on greased baking sheet. Put a small slit in top of turnover. Repeat rolling and filling until all dough is used. Bake for 15 minutes, until turnovers are browned and filling is translucent. Allow to cool.

Combine topping ingredients. Mix until smooth. Drizzle over top of turnovers.

Makes 4–6 turnovers. Serves 6.

Calories	324	Protein	1 g
Fat	18 g	Fiber	5 g
Cholesterol	1 mg	Sodium	196 mg
Carbohydrate	42 g		

Traditional Piecrust

Here is a really decent piecrust. I promise. However, please know that this crust can be a bit difficult to work with, especially if you are making a full top or lattice top for your pie. It can be beautiful—just look at the picture on the front of this book.

Ingredients

1/2 cup shortening
1/2 cup potato starch
3/4 cup cornstarch
1 teaspoon sugar
1 1/2 teaspoons baking powder
3 teaspoons xanthan gum
1/4 teaspoon baking soda
1/4 cup plus 1 tablespoon milk

Directions

Preheat oven to 400°. In medium bowl, combine all ingredients. Mix very well to remove all lumps. If dough will not stay together, blend in an extra tablespoon of milk. Roll out dough on floured surface or between two sheets of waxed paper. Circle of dough should be about 1 1/2 inches larger in diameter than pie plate. I personally prefer to use waxed paper for ease in placing dough into the pan.

Remove top sheet of waxed paper (if using) and place piecrust into pan. Trim excess dough and pinch edges at top of pie pan to form a pretty border.

If using a nonbaked filling, prick piecrust all over with a fork. Bake 10–14 minutes until crust is golden brown. Allow to cool.

If using a filling that will be baked, do not prebake piecrust.

Makes one 9- or 10-inch piecrust.

Calories	269	Protein	0 g
Fat	18 g	Fiber	4 g
Cholesterol	1 mg	Sodium	195 mg
Carbohydrate	28 g		

Sweet Pastry Crust

This thin crust is perfect with fresh fruits and tarts. It is used with the Apple Tart in this chapter, but other fresh fruits work well, too.

Ingredients

2 tablespoons shortening
1/3 cup sugar
2 tablespoons oil
1 egg yolk
1/2 teaspoon vanilla flavoring
1/3 cup potato starch
1/2 cup cornstarch
1/2 teaspoon xanthan gum
1/4 teaspoon salt
3 teaspoons water

Directions

Preheat oven to 350°. In medium bowl, combine shortening and sugar. Mix well. Add remaining ingredients and mix well to remove all lumps. Place dough into bottom of greased springform pan.

Top as desired, then bake until crust is light golden brown.

Calories	199	Protein	1 g
Fat	10 g	Fiber	1 g
Cholesterol	36 mg	Sodium	92 mg
Carbohydrate	28 g		

CHAPTER 9

Other Sweets

This probably was the most fun chapter to write. I felt as if I were bouncing around in my favorite shop that prepared everything just the way I liked them.

This chapter has a lot of good things in it. The Ice Cream Cones are fun to make and really good to eat. The Cheesecake is delicious. And the Apple Crisp is great with a scoop of ice cream.

There really is a lot of diversity in this chapter. Please leaf through it page by page. You will find something you've been missing!

Apple Crisp

I like a lot of Streusel Topping on my apple crisp, and this recipe has lots! There's plenty, even if you use a shallow pan. If you like less topping, halve the streusel recipe.

Streusel Topping

1/2 cup shortening
3/4 cup sugar
1/2 cup potato starch
3/4 cup cornstarch
2 teaspoons baking powder
1/2 teaspoon salt
1 1/2 teaspoons xanthan gum
1/4 cup milk
1/4 teaspoon cinnamon

Ingredients

5–6 medium apples, peeled, cored, chopped (about 5 cups)
1 1/2 tablespoons cornstarch
2 tablespoons sugar (use a bit more for tart apples)
1/4 teaspoon cinnamon

Directions

Preheat oven to 375°. In medium bowl, combine all Streusel Topping ingredients. Mix to form small clumpy pieces. If you overmix, you may simply break off small pieces of the topping to form small pieces. Set aside.

In large bowl, combine apples, cornstarch, sugar, and cinnamon. Toss to coat well. Put apple mixture into lightly greased pie plate or $1^1/_2$-quart casserole. Top with streusel mixture.

Bake 35 minutes, until apples are tender and streusel is browned.

Serves 6.

Calories	449	Protein	1 g
Fat	18 g	Fiber	5 g
Cholesterol	1 mg	Sodium	363 mg
Carbohydrate	75 g		

Apple Fritters

These old-fashioned treats are still delicious today! They have a light coating, are just a little sweet, and are sure to please.

Ingredients

2 eggs, separated
2/3 cup milk
2 teaspoons oil
1/4 teaspoon salt
1/4 teaspoon vanilla flavoring (optional)
2 teaspoons sugar
1/3 cup cornstarch
1/3 cup potato starch
1/8 teaspoon xanthan gum
1/4 teaspoon baking powder
5–6 large apples, peeled, cored, and sliced 1/3 inch thick (peel as you go to prevent discoloration)

For frying

1 cup shortening (preferred to oil in this use)

For topping

1/4 cup powdered sugar

Directions

In medium bowl, mix egg yolks, milk, and oil. Add all dry ingredients. Mix well to remove all lumps.

In separate bowl, beat egg whites to stiff peaks. Fold egg whites into batter. Incorporate well, but avoid beating.

Preheat oil to 375° in frying pan or skillet. Dip slices of apple into batter to coat well. Place slices in hot oil. Do not crowd. When medium golden brown, turn slices over. When equally browned on both sides, remove and drain on paper towels.

Sprinkle tops of slightly cooled fritters with powdered sugar.

Makes 8 servings.

Calories	266	Protein	2 g
Fat	16 g	Fiber	2 g
Cholesterol	55 mg	Sodium	110 mg
Carbohydrate	30 g		

Baked Custard

This is a traditional baked custard. If you don't care for nutmeg, leave it off.

Ingredients

4 eggs
1/4 cup sugar
1 teaspoon vanilla flavoring
2 cups milk
few pinches of nutmeg

To upgrade this tasty custard to a crème caramel, omit nutmeg and bake. Once cooled, sprinkle a little sugar on top of each custard, and melt the sugar with a small blow torch or under a broiler until appropriately browned.

Directions

Preheat oven to 350°. In medium bowl, combine eggs and sugar. Stir until eggs are fully mixed. Add vanilla flavoring and milk. Again, mix well until eggs are fully incorporated. Pour into individual ramekins or other single-serving, oven-safe dishes. Dust the top of each custard with nutmeg.

Place ramekins into larger metal baking pan. Fill this pan about half full with water. This will encourage a smooth, even texture in the custard. Bake for 45–50 minutes, until knife inserted in middle of custard tests clean.

Makes 4 servings.

Calories	184	Protein	10 g
Fat	7 g	Fiber	0 g
Cholesterol	222 mg	Sodium	124 mg
Carbohydrate	19 g		

Banana Pudding

Banana Pudding is my big brother's favorite dessert. While you must make all of the components from scratch, you will be richly rewarded.

Recommended cookies

1 batch Vanilla Wafers (35–40 will be used), (page 206)

Recommended pudding

1 recipe Vanilla Pudding (freshly made and still warm), (page 263)

Recommended topping

1 recipe Meringue (freshly made), (page 251)

Other ingredients

2 large or 3 medium bananas

Directions

Arrange a single layer of vanilla wafers on the sides and bottom of a medium ovenproof casserole or bowl ($1\frac{1}{2}$-quart). Slice 1 banana and arrange over top of Vanilla Wafers. Pour approximately $\frac{1}{2}$ of pudding over top of bananas. Smooth with a large spoon.

Make a second layer of vanilla wafers on top of the pudding. Again, make another layer of banana slices. Top with remaining pudding.

Place meringue over top of the pudding and to the very edges of the casserole. This will help prevent the meringue from shrinking. Use the back of a spoon to create decorative swirls or peaks in the meringue. Place pudding under broiler for a few minutes to brown meringue. Refrigerate.

Makes 8 servings.

Calories	284	Protein	5 g
Fat	9 g	Fiber	1 g
Cholesterol	38 mg	Sodium	161 mg
Carbohydrate	47 g		

Blueberry Cobbler

Cobblers are really easy to make, and this one is no exception. There is nothing fancy about the flavorings here, just lots of blueberry goodness.

Recommended biscuit dough

Sweet Biscuits (prepared, but not baked), (page 129)

For filling

4 cups blueberries, fresh or frozen
3/4 cup water
1/2 cup sugar
2 tablespoons cornstarch

Recommended topping (optional)

Whipped Cream (page 264) *or*
milk

Directions

Preheat oven to 375°. Prepare Sweet Biscuit Dough; set aside.

In medium saucepan, combine all filling ingredients. Mix well, being careful not to crush the berries. Cook until thickened. Pour filling into greased deep-dish pie plate or 2-quart casserole.

Drop biscuit dough by rounded tablespoonful on top of the filling. (Dough may be patted out and cut if a more polished look is desired.) Bake about 15 minutes, until and biscuits are lightly browned. Place servings on individual plates or bowls and top with Whipped Cream or milk as desired.

Makes 8 servings.

Calories	223	Protein	1 g
Fat	9 g	Fiber	3 g
Cholesterol	2 mg	Sodium	388 mg
Carbohydrate	36 g		

Cheesecake

Have you ever made a cheesecake only to hesitantly keep it in the oven longer, maybe a lot longer, than the recipe calls for? Or how about leaving it in after the oven is turned off? I've never been happy with either situation. So, I've fixed my concerns (and maybe yours, too). I simply keep the cheesecake in the oven until it is set—no guessing, no nervousness, just great cheesecake!

Suggested crust

Cookie Crumb Crust (page 217) *or*
Sweet Pastry Crust (page 234)

Ingredients

3/4 cup sugar
3 8-ounce packages cream cheese
2 teaspoons vanilla flavoring
1 cup sour cream
2 tablespoons cornstarch
4 eggs

Directions

Preheat oven to 350°. Make crust and put in lightly-greased springform pan. Set aside.

Cream sugar and cream cheese until smooth. Slowly add all other ingredients except eggs. Mix well. Add eggs and mix until fully incorporated. Do not overbeat.

Have you ever seen a cheesecake that has sunk in the middle? This is caused by baking the cake at too high a temperature. Cheesecake should not be rushed.

Pour batter into pan. Place pan on top of baking sheet, as mixture may "weep" a bit during baking. Bake 15 minutes. Reduce heat to 225°. Bake an additional 90–120 minutes, until set and knife inserted in middle tests clean.

Cake is best refrigerated overnight.

Makes 10 rich servings.

Calories	462	Protein	8 g
Fat	37 g	Fiber	0 g
Cholesterol	178 mg	Sodium	235 mg
Carbohydrate	26 g		

Chocolate Cheesecake

Here is a lovely, rich, chocolate cheesecake adapted from my original Cheesecake recipe. I accidentally used these two chocolates together when trying a cheesecake recipe some time ago and was surprised by the terrific results. Accordingly, the accidental chocolate combination is used for your enjoyment.

Recommended crust

Cookie Crumb Crust (page 217) *or*
Sweet Pastry Crust (page 234)

Ingredients

3/4	cup sugar
3	8-ounce packages cream cheese
2	teaspoons vanilla flavoring
1	cup sour cream
2	tablespoons cornstarch
4	ounces semisweet chocolate chips (2/3 cup)
2	ounces unsweetened chocolate
4	eggs

Directions

Preheat oven to 350°. Make crust and put in lightly-greased springform pan. Set aside.

Cream sugar and cream cheese until smooth. Slowly add all other ingredients except eggs and chocolates. Mix well. Set aside.

In microwaveable bowl or cup, melt semisweet chocolate chips and unsweetened chocolate. To melted chocolates, add a few tablespoons of cream cheese mixture. (Do not be concerned if chocolate should seize up—it will still be delicious.) Mix this chocolate mixture into the remaining cream cheese mixture. Add eggs and mix until fully incorporated. Do not overbeat.

Pour batter into pie pan. Place pan on top of baking sheet, as mixture may "weep" a bit during baking. Bake 15 minutes. Reduce heat to 225°. Bake an additional 90–120 minutes, until set and knife inserted in middle tests clean.

Cake is best refrigerated overnight.

Makes 10 ample servings.

Calories	548	Protein	9 g
Fat	44 g	Fiber	1 g
Cholesterol	178 mg	Sodium	237 mg
Carbohydrate	34 g		

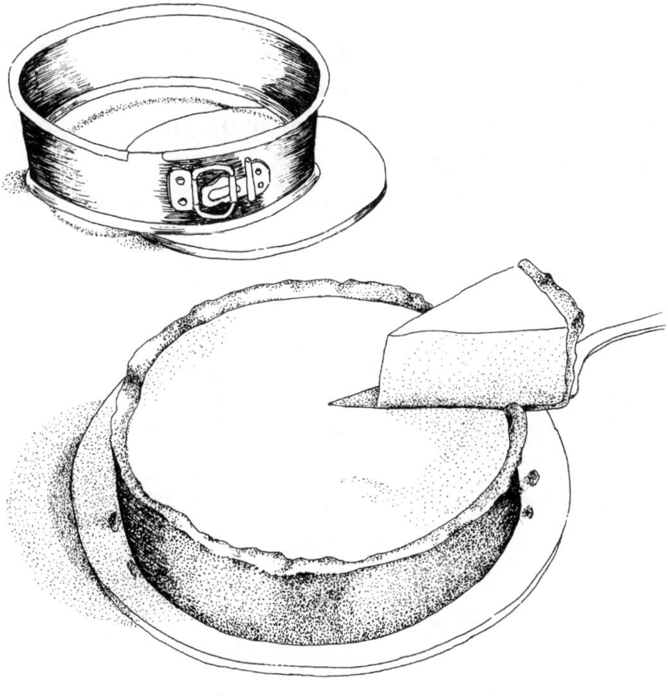

Chocolate Pudding

This is a really nice chocolate pudding. The chocolate flavor is intense when compared to prepared puddings. Use a bit less cocoa if you prefer a lighter chocolate taste. The egg adds richness and fullness to the pudding but may be omitted if needed.

Ingredients

2 cups milk
2 teaspoons vanilla flavoring
1/2 cup sugar
3 tablespoons cornstarch
1/4 cup cocoa
1 egg

Directions

In medium saucepan, combine all ingredients. Stir well to blend. Cocoa will seem to float on top of milk but will incorporate while warming. Over medium heat, stir constantly until mixture beings to thicken and boil.

Remove from heat and pour into 4 small serving dishes.

Makes 4 servings.

Calories	220	Protein	7 g
Fat	4 g	Fiber	0 g
Cholesterol	62 mg	Sodium	79 mg
Carbohydrate	38 g		

Meringue

I personally love large amounts of Meringue on top of a pie, but most pie recipes don't use as much as I'd prefer. In keeping with the anticipated, here's a regular-size recipe. If you want more, use the taller version. I also give the option of using dried egg whites in this recipe, because they are pasteurized. It is really difficult to gauge whether or not meringue has reached a safely baked temperature. If you are sure your eggs are safe, you can use the fresh alternative.

Ingredients for an average pie

3 egg whites *or*
6 teaspoons Just Whites and 1/4 cup plus 2 tablespoons water
1/3 cup sugar
scant 1/2 teaspoon cream of tartar
1/4 teaspoon vanilla flavoring

Ingredients for a taller pie

6 egg whites *or*
4 tablespoons Just Whites and 3/4 cup water
2/3 cup sugar
scant 1 teaspoon cream of tartar
1/2 teaspoon vanilla flavoring

Directions

In medium bowl, combine all ingredients. Mix with a whisk or mixer until stiff peaks are formed. Meringue should not slide in the bottom of the bowl. If it does, beat it a bit longer.

Calories	51	Protein	2 g
Fat	0 g	Fiber	0 g
Cholesterol	0 mg	Sodium	27 mg
Carbohydrate	11 g		

Peach Cobbler

Nothing beats our Peach Cobbler in the summer with a scoop of ice cream melting over the top while the cobbler is still hot. Please use the freshest peaches you can find—it really matters.

Recommended dough

Sweet Biscuits (prepared, but not baked), (page 129)

For filling

4 large peaches, peeled, pitted, and sliced (about 4 cups)
1/4 cup sugar
1/2 cup water
2 tablespoons cornstarch
1/2 teaspoon cinnamon

Recommended toppings (optional)

Whipped Cream (page 264) *or*
ice cream

Directions

Preheat oven to 375°. Prepare biscuit dough, but do not bake. Set aside.

For fruit filling, in medium saucepan, combine peaches, sugar, water, cornstarch, and cinnamon. Cook over medium heat until thick. Stir well, but be careful not to damage fruit. Pour fruit into a casserole dish for baking.

Drop biscuit dough by rounded tablespoonful on top of the filling. (Dough may be patted out and cut if a more polished look is desired.)

Bake about 15 minutes, until biscuits are lightly browned. Place servings on individual plates or bowls and top with Whipped Cream or ice cream as desired.

Makes 8 servings.

Calories	182	Protein	1 g
Fat	9 g	Fiber	3 g
Cholesterol	2 mg	Sodium	383 mg
Carbohydrate	25 g		

Rice Pudding

In this recipe, it's nice to use basmati or jasmine rice, which make for a more fragrant, subtle pudding. If you don't use either of these rices, short-grain rice will do just fine.

Ingredients

1/2 cup rice cooked in 1 cup water *or*
1 cup leftover rice
2 cups milk
1/4 cup sugar
4 eggs
1/2 teaspoon cinnamon
1 teaspoon vanilla flavoring
1/4 teaspoon salt
1 teaspoon cornstarch

Directions

In medium saucepan, cook rice in water until tender, about 15 minutes. Remove from heat. To cooked rice, add remaining ingredients and stir well.

Return to low heat (or place mixture in double boiler), stirring constantly. Cook until mixture begins to thicken. Do not overheat or the eggs will curdle and the liquid will become watery.

Pour mixture into serving dish(es) and refrigerate. Once cooled, it is good to cover the pudding with plastic wrap to keep other flavors in the refrigerator from being absorbed by the pudding. It also helps to prevent a "skin" from forming on the top of the pudding.

Makes 6 servings.

Calories	159	Protein	8 g
Fat	5 g	Fiber	0 g
Cholesterol	148 mg	Sodium	172 mg
Carbohydrate	20 g		

Crepes

Crepes are versatile, tasty, and quick to make. This recipe is basic, enhanced with a bit of sugar and/or jam.

Ingredients

3 eggs
1 tablespoon cornstarch
1 tablespoon potato starch
3 tablespoons milk
pinch of salt
1/4 teaspoon vanilla flavoring (optional, but nice)

For topping

1/4 cup jam *and/or*
2 tablespoons sugar

Directions

In small-medium bowl, combine all ingredients. Mix until eggs are fully incorporated and no lumps remain.

Heat a 5- or 6-inch frying pan (I use an omelet pan) to medium heat. Move pan from heat, spray with nonstick spray or add a bit of butter, and return to heat.

Pour 1/8 to 1/4 cup batter into pan. Swirl pan to move batter over bottom of pan until batter begins to set.

Cook about 1 minute, until batter is fully set. Flip crepe over and cook on other side for about 30 seconds.

While still warm, fill crepes with a bit of jam, fold in thirds, and top with a small amount of sugar. Serve warm if possible.

Makes 5–6 crepes. Serves 2.

Calories	308	Protein	10 g
Fat	8 g	Fiber	0 g
Cholesterol	321 mg	Sodium	177 mg
Carbohydrate	50 g		

Funnel Cake

Do you miss walking around carnivals eating this odd-looking confection? These are light and delicious. They are easiest to make if you have a squeeze bottle, like the kind often used for mustard. Otherwise, a big spoon will do.

Ingredients

1/2 cup potato starch
1/2 cup cornstarch
2 tablespoons sugar
1/4 teaspoon baking soda
1 teaspoon baking powder
1/2 teaspoon xanthan gum
1/2 teaspoon vanilla flavoring
pinch of salt
1 egg
3/4 teaspoon vinegar
3/4 cup milk

For frying

2 cups vegetable oil

For topping

1/2 cup powdered sugar

Directions

Preheat oil to 375°. In medium bowl, combine all dry ingredients. Add egg and vinegar. Slowly add milk, mixing well to remove all lumps.

Pour batter into squeeze bottle. Squeeze up to 1/3 cup batter into hot oil to form criss-crossing circles and ovals. If you have no squeeze bottle, slowly drop batter from spoon in similar shapes.

Cook until lightly browned. Turn to brown other side as well. Remove and drain on paper towels. While still warm, sprinkle powdered sugar on top.

Makes 6 funnel cakes. Serves 6.

Calories	252	Protein	2 g
Fat	12 g	Fiber	1 g
Cholesterol	38 mg	Sodium	192 mg
Carbohydrate	35 g		

Ice Cream Cones

OK, this recipe is here because I am a mom. Only a parent would risk burning his or her hands to shape an ice cream cone for their child, right? These ice cream cones are yummy; they taste like a light version of a sugar cone.

Ingredients

2	egg whites
1/2	cup sugar
	pinch of salt
1/4	teaspoon vanilla flavoring
1/4	teaspoon xanthan gum
1/4	cup cornstarch
1/4	cup potato starch
2	tablespoons shortening
1–3	tablespoons water

Directions

Mix egg whites until frothy. Mix in all other ingredients. Be sure no lumps remain.

Pour approximately 1 1/2 tablespoons batter into greased, hot pan. I use an omelet pan. Swirl to distribute the batter over the bottom of the pan. The thinner the better. Cook until golden brown on the bottom. Turn and cook until other side is golden brown. This will take several minutes on each side.

Carefully (very carefully) remove from pan and shape into traditional cone shape. Place seam side down to cool.

Makes about 8 cones.

Calories	109	Protein	1 g
Fat	3 g	Fiber	0 g
Cholesterol	0 mg	Sodium	31 mg
Carbohydrate	20 g		

Streusel

Do you like streusel on top of ice cream? Do you like streusel on top of pie? How about on top of a fruit crisp? This recipe is a bit different from traditional streusel, for obvious gluten-free reasons. But it is good! It's used on the Apple Crisp recipe and the Peach Streusel Pie recipe in this book.

Ingredients

1/2 cup shortening
3/4 cup sugar
1/2 cup potato starch
3/4 cup cornstarch
2 teaspoons baking powder
1/2 teaspoon salt
1 1/2 teaspoons xanthan gum
1/4 cup milk
1/4 teaspoon cinnamon

Directions

Preheat oven to 375°. In medium bowl, combine all ingredients. Mix to form small clumpy pieces. If you overmix, you may simply break off small pieces of the topping to form small pieces.

Streusel may be baked by itself to use as an ice cream topping or used to top pies, tarts, and crisps.

Calories	353	Protein	0 g
Fat	18 g	Fiber	2 g
Cholesterol	1 mg	Sodium	362 mg
Carbohydrate	50 g		

Vanilla Pudding

This vanilla pudding is rich, but not too rich. It's too bad that so many people use boxed mixes for pudding. They really don't compare. The egg is included for color and richness, but it may be omitted if desired.

Ingredients

2 cups milk
2 teaspoons vanilla flavoring
1/2 cup sugar
3 tablespoons cornstarch
pinch of salt
1 egg

Directions

In medium saucepan, combine all ingredients. Stir well to blend. Over medium heat, stir constantly until mixture begins to thicken and boil.

Remove from heat and pour into 4 small serving dishes.

Makes 4 servings.

Calories	199	Protein	6 g
Fat	4 g	Fiber	0 g
Cholesterol	62 mg	Sodium	111 mg
Carbohydrate	36 g		

Whipped Cream

Whipped Cream is just so good! Enjoy this on pies, ice cream, tarts, or even in your coffee.

Ingredients

1 cup heavy cream

2 tablespoons powdered sugar (more if you prefer)

1/2 teaspoon vanilla flavoring

Directions

In medium bowl, combine all ingredients. Using a whisk or mixer, beat until soft peaks form.

Makes 8 1/4-cup servings.

Calories	111	Protein	1 g
Fat	11 g	Fiber	0 g
Cholesterol	42 mg	Sodium	12 mg
Carbohydrate	2 g		

APPENDIX

Gluten-Free Resources

National Gluten-Free Support Groups

American Celiac Society
58 Musano Court
West Orange, NJ 07052
201-325-8837

Celiac Disease Foundation
13251 Ventura Boulevard, Suite 3
Studio City, CA 91604
818-990-2354

Celiac Sprue Association/USA Inc.
P.O. Box 31700
Omaha, NE 68131-0700
402-558-0600
Web site: www.csaceliacs.org

The Gluten Intolerance Group of North America
15110 10th Avenue SW, Suite A
Seattle, WA 98166-1820
206-246-6652
fax: 206-246-6531
E-mail: gig@accessone.com

To locate a local support group, contact one of the national support groups and/or refer to this terrific Web site: www.celiac.com

Gluten-Free Mail-Order Suppliers

In the last 10 years, the availability of gluten-free foods and the number of gluten-free food manufacturers have grown tremendously. Unfortunately, I do not personally know all of these suppliers. However, each one has been contacted for the product line and, more specifically, their ability to provide the ingredients used in these recipes.

Arrowhead Mills
P.O. Box 2059
Hereford, TX 79045
800-749-0730

Products: many gluten-free flours found in grocery stores and health food stores

Authentic Foods
1850 W. 169th St., Suite B
Gardena, CA 90247
800-806-4737
fax: 310-366-6938
Web site: www.authenticfoods.com

Products: mixes, bean flours, natural flavors, gums

Dietary Specialties
865 Centennial Ave.
Piscataway, NJ 08854
1-888-MENU123 or 716-263-2787
Web site: www.dietspec.com

Products: baking mixes, breads, pastas, crackers, cookies, condiments, extracts, and snacks

Ener-G Foods
P.O. Box 84487
5960 1st Ave. South
Seattle, WA 98124-5787
800-331-5222
E-mail: samii@ener-g.com

Products: bakery products, mixes, flours, flavorings, xanthan gum, guar gum, and much more

Food for Life Baking Co., Inc.
2991 E. Doherty St.
Corona, CA 91719
800-797-5090
Web site: www.food-for-life.com

Products: breads

Foods by George
530 Broad St.
Glen Rock, NJ 07452
201-612-9700

Products: frozen bakery and pasta products

F. T. Loa Cookies
551 Valley Road, Suite 124
Upper Montclair, NJ 07043
888-366-8709
Web site: www.ftloacookies.com
E-mail: loa@ftloacookies.com

Products: cookies and "brownys"

G! Foods
3536 17th St.
San Francisco, CA 94110
415-255-2139
fax: 415-863-3359
Web site: www.g-foods.com

Products: breakfast bars and cookies

Gillian's Foods Inc.
462 Proctor Ave.
Revere, MA 02151-5730
781-286-4095
Web site: www.GilliansFoods.com
E-mail: R357BOBO@aol.com
fax: 781-286-1933

Products: breads, rolls, chicken parmesan

The Gluten Free Cookie Jar
P.O. Box 52
Trevose, PA 19053
215-355-9403
1-800-GLUTEN-0
Web site: www.glutenfreecookiejar.com
fax: 215-355-7991

Products: cookies

Gluten-Free Delights
P.O. Box 284
Cedar Falls, IA 50613
1-888-403-1806
319-266-7167

fax: 319-268-7355
Web site: www.glutenfreedelights.com

Products: breads, cookies, deserts

The Gluten-Free Mall
Web site: www.glutenfreemall.com

Products: one-stop-shopping bringing together a growing number of gluten-free foods manufacturers

Gluten Free Essentials
6638 Gilardi Road
Boonsboro, MD 21713
301-432-859
877-432-8595
Fax 301-432-4373
Web site: www.gfessentials.com
E-mail: eryberg@aol.com

Products: xanthan gum, guar gum, karaya gum, carrageenan (special formulation, gum substitute), flavorings, spices, English muffin rings, pastry bags, cookbooks. This company provides ingredients and supplies suggested in this book.

The Gluten-Free Pantry
P.O. Box 840
Glastonbury, CT 06033
860-633-3826
order line: 800-291-8386
fax: 860-633-6853
Web site: www.glutenfree.com
E-mail: pantry@glutenfree.com

Products: baking mixes, pastas, cookies, soups, cookbooks, vanilla, xanthan gum, guar gum, and much more

Gulpener
100 Shillhammer Road
Jericho, VT 05465
800-958-7678
fax: 802-899-4678

Products: vinegars and mustards

HeartyMix
1231 Madison Hill Road
Rahway, NJ 07065
732-382-3010

Products: baking mixes

Jowar Foods, Inc.
113 Hickory St.
Hereford, TX 79045
806-363-9070
fax: 806-364-1984
Web site: www.jowar.com

Products: mixes and sorghum flour

King Arthur Flour
P.O. Box 876
Norwich, VT 05055
800-827-6836
Web site: www.kingarthurflour.com

Products: flours and xanthan gum

Miss Roben's Dietary Foods
P.O. Box 1434
Frederick, MD 21702

800-891-0083
Web site: www.missroben.com
E-mail: missroben@msn.com

Products: snacks, pastas, baking mixes, flours, xanthan gum, guar gum, vitamins, books, egg and milk substitutes

Nancy's Natural Foods
266 NW First Ave.
Canby, OR 97013
877-862-4457
E-mail: nnfoods@juno.com *or* roy_armour@mentorg.com

Products: bakery goods, flours, milk powders and substitutes, books, bulk foods, natural flavors, condiments, and more

Natural Feast Corp.
435 Coggeshall St.
P.O. Box 50158
New Bedford, MA 02745
508-984-4230

Products: gourmet pies

Oakland Dietetic Bakery
P.O. Box 180302
Utica, MI 48318-0302
800-815-6280
Web site: www.oaklanddieteticbakery.com
E-mail: jjfb@flash.net

Products: cookies

Old Windmill
5014 16th Avenue, Suite 202
Brooklyn, NY 11204
800-653-3791

Pamela's Products
335 Allerton Ave.
San Francisco, CA 94080
650-952-4546
fax: 650-742-6643
Web site: www.pamelasproducts.com

Products: mixes, cookies, biscotti

The Really Great Food Co.
P.O. Box 319
Malverne, NY 11565
516-593-5587
800-593-5377
Web site: www.reallygreatfood.com

Products: baking mixes, flours, xanthan gum

Special Foods
9207 Shotgun Court
Springfield, VA 22153
703-644-0991
fax: 703-644-1006
Web site: www.specialfoods.com
E-mail: kslimak@ix.netcom.com

Products: flours

Additional Resources for the Gluten-Free Community

Gluten-Free Living is a bimonthly magazine for living without gluten. They may be reached at:

Gluten-Free Living
P.O. Box 105
Hastings-on-the-Hudson, NY 10706

The Internet has become a very valuable tool for the gluten-intolerant individual. From the Web, foods and baking supplies can be ordered, new medical findings and information can be accessed, and connections to support areas can be located. While a simple search on the Web of "gluten intolerance" will yield many, many resources, I have listed a few of my favorites to get you started:

www.celiac.com
www.foodallergy.org
www.allergy.co.uk
www.niddk.nih.gov/health/digest/pubs/celiac/index.htm
www.glutenfreeinfo.com
www.ozemail.com.au/~coeliac/gluten-free_recipes.html
www.forums.delphi.com/celiac/start

Index

A

All-Purpose Loaf, 76
Angel Food Cake, 136–137
  chocolate, 146–147
Apple
  crisp, 236–237
  fritters, 238–239
  muffins, 110–111
  pie, 208–209
  tart, 216
Apple cider vinegar, 6
Applesauce Quick Bread, 126

B

Bagels, 14–15
Baked Custard, 240–241
Baking powder, 3
Baking soda, 3
Banana
  bread, 112–113
  muffins, 114–115
  pudding, 242–243
Basic Pancakes, 29
Beef Vegetable Soup, 67
Bernbaum, Rose, 146
Biscuits, 75
  cinnamon-raisin, 22–23
  sweet, 129
Blueberry
  cobbler, 244–245
  muffins, 116–117
  tart, 210–211
Boston Cream Pie, 138–139
Bread machines, 8
Breads, 73–74. *See also* Quick breads
  all-purpose loaf, 76–77
  biscuits, 75
  buttermilk loaf, 78–79
  cheese straws, 82–83
  chocolate bread, 92–93
  cinnamon loaf, 84–85
  cinnamon rolls, 86–87
  cornbread, 88–89
  cottage dill bread, 90–91
  dinner rolls, 104
  egg bread loaf, 94–95
  English muffins, 96–97
  focaccia, 98–99
  hot cross buns, 100–101
  pizza crust, 102–103
  sourdough loaf, 106–107
Bread Sticks, 80–81
Breakfast, 13
  bagels, 14–15
  buttermilk pancakes, 16–17
  chipped beef gravy, 20–21
  cinnamon-raisin biscuits, 22–23
  coffee cake, 24–25
  Danish, 26–27
  doughnuts, cake, 18–19
  doughnuts, raised, 32–33
  French toast, 28
  muffins, sour cream, 34–35
  pancakes, 29

Breakfast, *continued*
pancakes, sourdough, 36–37
sausage gravy, 30–31
streusel cake, 40–41
waffles, light, everyday, 39
waffles, special, 38
Brown sugar, 3
Brownies, 170–171
cheesecake, 174–175
Burnt-edge Wafers, 172–173
Butter, 3
Buttercream Icing, 135
Buttermilk Loaf, 78–79
Buttermilk Pancakes, 16–17

C

Cake doughnuts, 18–19
Cakes, 133–134. *See also* Sweets
angel food cake, 136–137
baking time for, 134
Boston cream pie, 138–139
buttercream icing, 135
carrot cake, 140–141
chocolate angel food cake, 146–147
chocolate buttercream icing, 142
chocolate cake, 144–145
chocolate cake, petite, 153
chocolate cake, simply sinful, 160–161
chocolate pound cake, 143
chocolate velvet icing, 148–149
gingerbread, 150–151
pecan cake, 152
pineapple upside-down cake, 156–157
red velvet cake, 158–159
spice snacking cake, 162–163
sponge cake, 164–165
velvet icing, 166–167
yellow cake, 168
yellow cake, petite, 154
Carrageenan, 10
Carrot Cake, 140–141
Celiac support groups, 1, 265–266
Cheese, 4–5
and ham pocket pies, 54–55
straws, 82–83
Cheesecake, 246–247
brownies, 174–175
chocolate, 248–249
Cherry Pie, 212–213
Chicken
breast, with wine and mushrooms, 46–47
fried, 52–53
marinated grilled, 56
pot pie, 48–49
rice soup, 44–45
Chili, 50–51
Chipped Beef Gravy, 20–21
Chocolate Bread, 92–93
Chocolate cake
angel food, 146–147
cheesecake, 248–249
petite, 153
pound cake, 143
simply sinful, 160–161
traditional, 144–145
Chocolate Chip Cookies, 176–177
Chocolate Cookies, Double, 182–183
Chocolate Drops, 178–179
Chocolate Meringue Pie, 214–215
Chocolate Pudding, 250
Chocolate Velvet Icing, 148–149

Cinnamon
loaf, 84–85
and raisin biscuits, 22–23
rolls, 86–87
Coffee cake, 24–25
Cookies, 169
brownies, 170–171
burnt-edge wafers, 172–173
cheesecake brownies, 174–175
chocolate chip cookies, 176–177
chocolate drops, 178–179
double chocolate cookies, 182–183
gingersnaps, 184–185
ladyfingers, 186–187
lemon cookie bars, 188–189
lemon sugar cookies, 190–191
peanut butter cookies, 192–193
pecan meringues, 181
raisin spice cookies, 194–195
rolled sugar cookies, 196–197
shortbread cookies, 198–199
snickerdoodles, 200–201
spritz, 202–203
sugar cookies, 180
toffee bars, 204–205
vanilla wafers, 206
Cornbread
version 1, 88
version 2, 89
Cornstarch, 2
Cottage Dill Loaf, 90–91
Cranberry Orange Bread, 118–119
Crepes, 256–257
Crispy Sugar Cookies, 180
Custard
baked, 240–241
pie, 218

D

Dairy foods, 4–5, 9
Desserts. *See* Cakes; Pies and tarts; Sweets
Dinner and lunch, 43
beef vegetable soup, 67
chicken breast with wine and mushrooms, 46–47
chicken pot pie, 48–49
chicken rice soup, 44–45
chili, 50–51
fried chicken, 52–53
ham and cheese pocket pies, 54–55
marinated grilled chicken, 56
meat loaf, 57
onion rings, 58
pizza, 62–63
pork scallopini, 60–61
quiche, 64–65
roast beef with gravy, 59
seafood crepes, 68–69
shepherd's pie, 70–71
stuffing, 66
Double Chocolate Cookies, 182–183
Doughnuts
cake, 18–19
raised, 32–33

E

Egg Bread Loaf, 94–95
Egg(s), 5, 10
quiche, 64–65

English Muffins, 96–97
Equipment, 7–8

F

Fats, 3
Flavorings, 5–6
Flours, 2
Focaccia, 98–99
French Toast, 28
Fried Chicken, 52–53
Fritters, apple, 238–239
Frosting. *See* Icing
Fruits, 7. *See also* specific fruit
  apple crisp, 236–237
  apple fritters, 238–239
  apple muffins, 110–111
  apple pie, 208–209
  apple tart, 216
  banana bread, 112–113
  banana muffins, 114–115
  banana pudding, 242–243
  blueberry cobbler, 244–245
  blueberry muffins, 116–117
  blueberry tart, 210–211
  cherry pie, 212–213
  cranberry orange bread, 118–119
  peach cobbler, 252–253
  peach streusel pie, 224–225
  pineapple upside-down cake, 156–157
  strawberry pie, 228–229
  strawberry shortcake, 128
Funnel Cake, 258–259

G

Gingerbread, 150–151
Gingersnaps, 184–185
Gluten-Free Living magazine, 272–273
Gluten-free mail-order suppliers, 2, 266–272
Gluten-free support groups, 1, 265–266
Guar gum, 3–4, 10

H

Ham and Cheese Pocket Pies, 54–55
Honey, 3
Hot Cross Buns, 100–101
Hush puppies
  savory, 127
  sweet, 132

I

Ice Cream Cones, 260–261
Icing
  buttercream, 135
  chocolate buttercream, 142
  chocolate velvet, 148–149
  velvet, 166–167

J

Jane's Krazy Mixed-Up Salt, 6, 81, 99

K

Key Lime Pie, 220–221

L

Ladyfingers, 186–187
Leavening, 3

Lemon
cookie bars, 188–189
meringue pie, 222–223
sugar cookies, 190–191
Light Everyday Waffles, 39
Lunch and dinner, 43
beef vegetable soup, 67
chicken breast with wine and mushrooms, 46–47
chicken pot pie, 48–49
chicken rice soup, 44–45
chili, 50–51
fried chicken, 52–53
ham and cheese pocket pies, 54–55
marinated grilled chicken, 56
meat loaf, 57
onion rings, 58
pizza, 62–63
pork scallopini, 60–61
quiche, 64–65
roast beef with gravy, 59
seafood crepes, 68–69
shepherd's pie, 70–71
stuffing, 66

M

Mail-order suppliers, 2, 266–272
Margarine, 3
Marinated Grilled Chicken, 56
Measuring cups/spoons, 8
Meats, 7. *See also* Chicken
chipped beef gravy, 20–21
ham and cheese pocket pies, 54–55
meat loaf, 57
pork scallopini, 60–61
roast beef with gravy, 59
sausage gravy, 30–31
shepherd's pie, 70–71
Meringue, 251
Milk, 4, 9
Muffins
apple, 110–111
banana, 114–115
blueberry, 116–117
pumpkin spice, 124–125
sour cream breakfast, 34–35

N

Nuts, 5–6
nut bread, 120–121
peanut butter cookies, 192–193
pecan cake, 152
pecan meringues, 181
pecan pie, 226–227

O

Onion Rings, 58

P

Pancakes
basic, 29
buttermilk, 16–17
sourdough, 36–37
Peach
cobbler, 252–253
streusel pie, 224–225
Peanut Butter Cookies, 192–193
Pecan
cake, 152
meringues, 181
pie, 226–227
Petite Chocolate Cake, 153
icing for, 166–167

Petite Yellow Cake, 154
Piecrust
  cookie crumb crust, 217
  sweet pastry crust, 234
  traditional, 232–233
Pies and tarts, 207. *See also* Sweets
  apple pie, 208–209
  apple tart, 216
  blueberry tart, 210–211
  cherry pie, 212–213
  chocolate meringue pie, 214–215
  custard pie, 218
  key lime pie, 220–221
  lemon meringue pie, 222–223
  peach streusel pie, 224–225
  pecan pie, 226–227
  pumpkin pie, 219
  strawberry pie, 228–229
  turnovers, 230–231
Pineapple Upside-Down Cake, 156–157
Pizza, 62–63
  crust, 102–103
Pork Scallopini, 60–61
Potato starch, 2
Pound Cake, 155
  chocolate, 143
Pudding
  banana, 242–243
  chocolate, 250
  rice, 254–255
  vanilla, 263
Pumpkin
  bread, 122–123
  pie, 219
  spice muffins, 124–125

Q

Quiche, 64–65
Quick breads, 109
  apple muffins, 110–111
  applesauce quick bread, 126
  banana bread, 112–113
  banana muffins, 114–115
  biscuits, sweet, 129
  blueberry muffins, 116–117
  cranberry orange bread, 118–119
  hush puppies, 127
  nut bread, 120–121
  pumpkin bread, 122–123
  pumpkin spice muffins, 124–125
  strawberry shortcake, 128
  zucchini bread, 130–131

R

Raised Doughnuts, 32–33
Raisin Spice Cookies, 194–195
Red Velvet Cake, 158–159
  icing for, 166–167
Resources, gluten-free
  author's favorite Web sites, 273
  Gluten-Free Living magazine, 272–273
  mail-order suppliers, 2, 266–272
  support groups, 1, 265–266
Rice, 6
  chicken rice soup, 44–45
  pudding, 254–255
Roast Beef with Gravy, 59
Rolled Sugar Cookies, 196–197

Rolls
cinnamon, 86–87
Danish, 26–27
dinner, 104–105

S

Salt, Jane's Krazy Mixed-Up, 6, 81, 99
Sausage gravy, 30–31
Savory Hush Puppies, 127
Seafood Crepes, 68–69
Shepherd's Pie, 70–71
Shortbread Cookies, 198–199
Simply Sinful Chocolate Cake, 160–161
Snickerdoodles, 200–201
Soups
beef vegetable, 67
chicken rice, 44–45
Sour Cream Breakfast Muffins, 34–35
Sourdough Loaf, 106–107
Sourdough Pancakes, 36–37
Special Waffles, 38
Spice Snacking Cake, 162–163
Spices and herbs, 6
Sponge Cake, 164–165
Spritz cookies, 202–203
Stabilizers and gums, 3–4
Storage of gluten-free baked goods, 10
Strawberry
pie, 228–229
shortcake, 128
Streusel, 262
Streusel Cake, 40–41
Stuffing, 66
Substitutions, 9–10
Sugar cookies
crispy, 180
lemon, 190–191
Sugars, 3
Support groups, 1, 265–266
Sweet Biscuits, 129
Sweet Pastry Crust, 234
Sweets. *See also* Cakes; Cookies; Pies and tarts
apple crisp, 236–237
apple fritters, 238–239
banana pudding, 242–243
blueberry cobbler, 244–245
cheesecake, 246–247
chocolate cheesecake, 248–249
chocolate pudding, 250
crepes, 256–257
custard, baked, 240–241
funnel cake, 258–259
ice cream cones, 260–261
meringue, 251
peach cobbler, 252–253
rice pudding, 254–255
streusel, 262
vanilla pudding, 263
whipped cream, 264

T

Toffee Bars, 204–205
Traditional Piecrust, 232–233
Turnovers, 230–231

V

Vanilla Pudding, 263
Vanilla Wafers, 206
Vegetables, 7
beef vegetable soup, 67
chicken pot pie, 48–49

Vegetables, *continued*
onion rings, 58
shepherd's pie, 70–71
Velvet Icing, 166–167
Vinegar, 6

W

Waffles
light, everyday, 39
special, 38
Web sites, gluten-free, 1–2
Whipped Cream, 264
Wine, 6, 9

X

Xanthan gum, 3–4, 10

Y

Yeast, 3, 74
Yellow Cake, 168
petite, 154

Z

Zucchini Bread, 130–131

International Conversion Chart

These are not exact equivalents: they have been slightly rounded to make measuring easier.

Liquid Measurements

American	*Imperial*	*Metric*	*Australian*
2 tablespoons (1 oz.)	1 fl. oz.	30 ml	1 tablespoon
1/4 cup (2 oz.)	2 fl. oz.	60 ml	2 tablespoons
1/3 cup (3 oz.)	3 fl. oz.	80 ml	1/4 cup
1/2 cup (4 oz.)	4 fl. oz.	125 ml	1/3 cup
2/3 cup (5 oz.)	5 fl. oz.	165 ml	1/2 cup
3/4 cup (6 oz.)	6 fl. oz.	185 ml	2/3 cup
1 cup (8 oz.)	8 fl. oz.	250 ml	3/4 cup

Spoon Measurements

American	*Metric*
1/4 teaspoon	1 ml
1/2 teaspoon	2 ml
1 teaspoon	5 ml
1 tablespoon	15 ml

Weights

US/UK	*Metric*
1 oz.	30 grams (g)
2 oz.	60 g
4 oz. (1/4 lb)	125 g
5 oz. (1/3 lb)	155 g
6 oz.	185 g
7 oz.	220 g
8 oz. (1/2 lb)	250 g
10 oz.	315 g
12 oz. (3/4 lb)	375 g
14 oz.	440 g
16 oz. (1 lb)	500 g
2 lbs	1 kg

Oven Temperatures

Farenheit	*Centigrade*	*Gas*
250	120	1/2
300	150	2
325	160	3
350	180	4
375	190	5
400	200	6
450	230	8